RISE OF ROME

REPUBLICAN ROME AT WAR

Written by Richard Bodley Scott, assisted by
Nik Gaukroger, James Hamilton and Paul
Robinson

First published in Great Britain in 2008 by Osprey Publishing Ltd.

© 2008 Osprey Publishing Ltd and Slitherine Software UK Ltd.

Osprey Publishing, Midland House, West Way, Botley, Oxford OX2 0PH, UK
443 Park Avenue South, New York, NY 10016, USA
E-mail: info@ospreypublishing.com

Slitherine Software UK Ltd., The White Cottage, 8 West Hill Avenue, Epsom, KT 19 8LE, UK
E-mail: info@slitherine.co.uk

A CIP catalogue record for this book is available from the British Library

ISBN: 978 1 84603 344 5

Rules system written by Richard Bodley Scott, Simon Hall, and Terry Shaw
Page layout by Myriam Bell
Index by Margaret Vaudrey
Typeset in Joanna Pro and Sleepy Hollow
Cover artwork by Peter Dennis
Photography supplied by Duncan MacFarlane – Wargames Illustrated
Page design features supplied by istockphoto.com
All images taken from Osprey publications © Osprey Publishing Ltd
Originated by PDQ Media, UK
Printed in China through Worldprint Ltd
Project management by JD McNeil & Simone Drinkwater
Technical management by Iain McNeil

08 09 10 11 12 12 11 10 9 8 7 6 5 4 3

FOR A CATALOGUE OF ALL BOOKS PUBLISHED BY OSPREY MILITARY
AND AVIATION PLEASE CONTACT:

NORTH AMERICA
Osprey Direct, c/o Random House Distribution Center, 400 Hahn Road,
Westminster, MD 21157
E-mail: info@ospreydirect.com

ALL OTHER REGIONS
Osprey Direct UK, P.O. Box 140 Wellingborough, Northants, NN8 2FA, UK
E-mail: info@ospreydirect.co.uk

FOR DETAILS OF ALL GAMES PUBLISHED BY SLITHERINE SOFTWARE UK LTD
email: info@Slitherine.co.uk

Osprey Publishing is supporting the Woodland Trust, the UK's leading woodland conservation charity, by funding the dedication of trees.

www.ospreypublishing.com

www.slitherine.com

CONTENTS

INTRODUCTION

Field of Glory is a historical miniature tabletop wargaming rules system for anyone interested in recreating the battles of the ancient and medieval eras. This army list companion is designed to be used alongside the Field of Glory rulebook, and covers the armies of Rome and its enemies and allies from 280 to 25 BC. During this period, Rome expanded from Italy to gain an empire which included the whole of the Mediterranean and its surrounding regions.

As you look at each army, you will find the following sections:

- Brief **historical notes** on the army, its wars, its famous generals, weapons and/or troop types.
- A ready-to-play **starter army** – just put it together and play a balanced small game.
- Instructions for building a **customized army** using our points system.
- A table with the full list of **compulsory** and **optional** troops.
- Supporting **illustrations** to give you a flavour of the period.
- Miniatures photographs.

Antesignani in combat with Acheaen Cavalry, Acheaen War, 146 BC, by Angus McBride.
Taken from Men-at-Arms 291: Republican Roman Army 200–104 BC.

4

By 280 BC, Rome had conquered its main Italian rivals, including the Etruscans and Samnites, controlling most of Italy by a network of forced alliances. The Greek city of Tarentum, in the heel of Italy, appealed to the Hellenistic king Pyrrhos of Epiros for aid against Rome. This was the first clash between the Roman legions and the Hellenistic pike phalanx. Although Pyrrhos won some hard-fought victories, he began to lose interest in the campaign and moved on elsewhere, allowing Rome to complete its control of southern Italy.

In 264 BC, a dispute between Rome and the Cathaginians over the city of Messina at the north-eastern tip of Sicily resulted in the First Punic War against Carthage. The war lasted until 241 BC, ending in Roman victory. Carthage was forced to surrender Sicily to Rome. In 237 BC, Corsica and Sardinia were also annexed by the Romans.

Carthage consoled itself by conquering a new empire in Spain. In 218 BC their general, Hannibal, instigated a Second Punic War. Hannibal invaded Italy and inflicted numerous severe defeats on the Roman armies. Things looked bleak for Rome. However, Hannibal never quite managed to capture Rome itself and the Romans fought back. They gradually managed to contain Hannibal in the far south of Italy, while in Spain their armies defeated other Carthaginians and conquered their Spanish empire. Eventually, the Romans invaded North Africa to threaten Carthage itself. Hannibal was recalled, but defeated at Zama in 202 BC. The former Carthaginian empire was reduced to modern Tunisia.

In 215 BC, during the Second Punic War, Rome first came into conflict with the Hellenistic kingdom of Macedon to the north of Greece, which led to four wars. After the fourth Macedonian war, in 148 BC, Macedon was annexed by Rome.

In 192 BC, an attempt by the eastern Hellenistic Seleucid kingdom to intervene in Greece provoked Roman intervention. The Seleucids were defeated in two battles, and lost their territories in Asia Minor, which were parceled out amongst Rome's allies.

In 149 BC, Rome found pretexts to declare war against Carthage again, and after the short Third Punic War destroyed Carthage and annexed her remaining territories.

In 133 BC, King Attalos III of Pergamon bequeathed his kingdom in western Asia Minor to Rome. Then in 88 BC, an attempt to check the expansionist ambitions of Mithridates of Pontus resulted in initial disaster for the Romans with the loss of the whole of Asia Minor and much of Greece. However, the Roman counterattack swiftly defeated the Pontic armies and swept Mithridates out of his newly conquered territories. Two further wars led to the final defeat of Mithridates in 63 BC and further territorial gains for Rome and her client allied kingdoms. The Syrian remnants of the Seleucid kingdom were annexed at this time.

From 58 to 51 BC, the Romans, under Julius Caesar, went on to conquer Gaul (modern France). Britain was also invaded briefly, but to no lasting effect. In 53 BC, an attempt to invade the Iranian Parthian kingdom in the east resulted in disaster at the battle of Carrhae.

From 49 BC, a series of civil wars wracked the Roman Empire. In the last phase of the wars, the Hellenistic Ptolemaic kingdom of Egypt became involved on the losing side, with the result that Egypt was annexed in 30 BC. Following this, Octavian, great-nephew and adoptive heir of Julius Caesar, was in sole control of the Roman world, becoming the first emperor, under the name of Augustus. By this time the Roman Empire included Italy, Spain, Gaul, North Africa, Greece, Asia Minor, Syria and Egypt. A series of small client kingdoms in the east acted as buffers against Parthia.

We have organized the army lists in approximately the order the states they cover first came into military contact with Rome.

MID-REPUBLICAN ROMAN

This list covers the armies of the Roman Republic from 280 to 105 BC — from the war against Pyrrhos of Epiros until the reforms of Marius. At the start of this period, Rome did not yet control the whole of Italy. By the end of the period, her empire had expanded to include not only the whole of Italy but also Sicily, Spain, Dalmatia, Greece and parts of Asia Minor and North Africa. In the meantime, epic wars had been fought and won against Epiros, Carthage, Macedon and the Seleucid Kingdom, as well as the Gallic, Spanish and Illyrian tribes.

THE LEGIONS

Rome's military success was based on her heavy infantry, the legions. According to Polybios, legions of this period were theoretically 4,200 strong, consisting of 1,200 *hastati*, 1,200 *principes*, 600 *triarii* and 1,200 lightly equipped *velites*. Each legion also had 300 cavalry. Allied *alae*, which were usually present in equal numbers to legions, were similarly organised but had three times as many cavalry. A legion would form up in three lines, the hastati in front, principes in the second line and triarii in the third. Each "line" consisted of

Roman Legionaries, Second Punic War, by Angus McBride © Osprey Publishing Ltd. Taken from Men-at-Arms 291: Republican Roman Army 200 – 104 BC.

maniples of 120 men, separated by intervals large enough for a maniple of the line behind to fill. This is the famous chequerboard formation, which gave the legion much greater flexibility in the advance than a solid phalanx as used by the Carthaginians and the Hellenistic kingdoms. It is uncertain how this formation worked in practice on contact with the enemy, as the gaps would appear to be a liability. However, as a battle group of 4 bases would represent 8 maniples at the normal troop representation scale, we do not need to worry about this level of detail. Instead, each battle group of hastati and principes is assumed to represent a number of maniples of both types in chequerboard formation.

Roman legionaries of this period carried a large oval shield (*scutum*). The semi-cylindrical shield of the 1st and early 2nd century AD had not yet come into use, nor had the *lorica segmentata* (body armour). Instead those able to afford it wore chain mail, while the poorer men were issued a small square bronze breastplate by the state. The hastati and principes fought with a heavy throwing spear (*pilum*) and short sword (*gladius*). The triarii still

carried the old thrusting spear (*hasta*). The hastati were drawn from the youngest and fittest men, the principes were experienced men in their prime, and the triarii were the veterans – less active but steady, and the last hope if anything went wrong.

Triarius

GENERAL SCIPIO AFRICANUS (235 – 183 BC)

Publius Cornelius Scipio Africanus Major was the Roman general who finally defeated the Carthaginian general Hannibal at Zama in 202 BC. His victories over lesser Carthaginian commanders in Spain had paved the way for the Roman invasion of Africa. He is held by some to have been a greater general than Hannibal. Nevertheless it could be said that he learned his trade from the exploits of the great Carthaginian. However, unlike Hannibal, he never lost a battle.

MID-REPUBLICAN ROMAN STARTER ARMY		
Commander-in-Chief	1	Troop Commander
Sub-commanders	2	2 x Troop Commander
Hastati & Principes	4 BGs	Each comprising 4 bases of legionaries: Superior, Armoured, Drilled Heavy Foot – Impact Foot, Skilled Swordsmen
Triarii	2 BGs	Each comprising 2 bases of legionaries: Elite, Armoured, Drilled Heavy Foot – Offensive Spearmen
Velites	2 BGs	Each comprising 4 bases of velites: Average, Unprotected, Drilled Light Foot – Javelins, Light Spear
Cavalry	2 BGs	Each comprising 4 bases of cavalry: Average, Armoured, Undrilled Cavalry – Light Spear, Swordsmen
Italian allied foot	1 BG	6 bases of medium foot javelinmen: Average, Protected, Drilled Medium Foot – Light Spear, Swordsmen
Camp	1	Fortified camp
Total	11 BGs	Camp, 8 mounted bases, 34 foot bases, 3 commanders

General Scipio Africanus was renowned as a merciful leader. (© C Hellier / AAA Collection Ltd.)

BUILDING A CUSTOMISED LIST USING OUR ARMY POINTS

Choose an army based on the maxima and minima in the list below. The following special instructions apply to this army:

- Commanders should be depicted as cavalry.
- Hastati, principes and triarii must be organised as legions: hastati and principes are brigaded together as battle groups. Depending on the size of army represented, a legion could be organised as 2 battle groups, each of 4 hastati and principes, and 1 battle group of 2 triarii, or as 2 battle groups, each of 8 hastati and principes, and 1 battle group of 4 triarii.
- It is recommended that each legion be deployed with its hastati and principes in front and its triarii in support behind.

- If part of a legion is upgraded, the whole legion must be upgraded.
- If part of a legion is downgraded, the whole legion including leves/velites must be downgraded.
- Apart from Italian allied foot, no more than 8 bases can be used from the optional troops list.
- Aitolian and Pergamene allies can be used together, otherwise only one nationality of allies can be used.
- Ligurians, thureophoroi, elephants, Numidian allies, Aitolian allies and Pergamene allies cannot be used before 202 BC.

Hastatus

8

MID-REPUBLICAN ROMAN

Territory Types: Agricultural, Developed, Hilly

C-in-C	Inspired Commander/Field Commander/Troop Commander				80/50/35	1	
Sub-commanders	Field Commander				50	0–2	
	Troop Commander				35	0–3	

Troop name	Troop Type				Capabilities		Points per base	Bases per BG	Total bases
	Type	Armour	Quality	Training	Shooting	Close Combat			
Core Troops									
Cavalry	Cavalry	Armoured	Average	Undrilled	-	Light Spear, Swordsmen	12	4–6	0–8
		Protected					9		
Legionaries:									
Hastati & Principes	Heavy Foot	Armoured	Average	Drilled	-	Impact Foot, Swordsmen	10	4–8	16–48
		Protected					8		
Triarii	Heavy Foot	Armoured	Superior	Drilled	-	Offensive Spearmen	13	2–4	1 per 4 Hastati & Principes
Leves or Velites	Light Foot	Unprotected	Average	Drilled	Javelins	Light Spear	4	4–8	1 per 2 Hastati & Principes
		Protected					5		
Upgrade veteran legionaries to:									
Hastati & Principes	Heavy Foot	Armoured	Superior	Drilled	-	Impact Foot, Skilled Swordsmen	14	4–8	0–16
		Protected					11		
Triarii	Heavy Foot	Armoured	Elite	Drilled	-	Offensive Spearmen	16	2–4	1 per 4 Hastati & Principes
Leves or Velites	Light Foot	Unprotected	Average	Drilled	Javelins	Light Spear	4	4–8	1 per 2 Hastati & Principes
		Protected					5		
Downgrade unenthusiastic allies, raw, slave or penal legionaries to:									
Hastati & Principes	Heavy Foot	Protected	Poor	Drilled	-	Impact Foot, Swordsmen	6	4–8	0–16
Triarii	Heavy Foot	Protected	Poor	Drilled	-	Offensive Spearmen	6	2–4	1 per 4 Hastati & Principes
Leves or Velites	Light Foot	Unprotected	Poor	Drilled	Javelins	Light Spear	2	4–8	1 per 2 Hastati & Principes
		Protected					3		
Fortified camp							24		1
Optional Troops									
Italian allied pedites extraordinarii	Medium Foot	Protected	Superior	Drilled	-	Light Spear, Swordsmen	9	4	0–4
		Armoured					12		
Other lighter equipped Italian allied infantry	Medium Foot	Protected	Average	Drilled	-	Light Spear, Swordsmen	7	6–8	0–12
			Poor				5		
Cretan archers	Light Foot	Unprotected	Superior	Drilled	Bow	-	6	4–6	0–6
Trallian or Syracusan slingers	Light Foot	Unprotected	Average	Undrilled	Sling	-	4	4–6	0–6
Spanish scutarii	Medium Foot	Protected	Average	Undrilled	-	Impact Foot, Swordsmen	7	4–6	0–6
Illyrian foot	Medium Foot	Protected	Average	Undrilled	-	Offensive Spearmen	7	4–6	0–6
Gallic foot	Heavy or Medium Foot	Protected	Average	Undrilled	-	Impact Foot, Swordsmen	7	4–6	0–6
Ligurian foot	Medium Foot	Protected	Average	Undrilled	-	Light Spear	5	4–6	0–6
Thureophoroi	Medium Foot or Heavy Foot	Protected	Average	Drilled	-	Offensive Spearmen	8	4–6	0–6
Numidian or Illyrian cavalry	Light Horse	Unprotected	Average	Undrilled	Javelins	Light Spear	7	4	0–4
Elephants	Elephants	-	Average	Undrilled	-	-	25	2	0–2
Allies									
Aitolian allies – Hellenistic Greek – See Field of Glory Companion 3: *Immortal Fire: Greek, Persian and Macedonian Wars.*									
Numidian allies									
Pergamene allies									
Spanish allies									

MID-REPUBLICAN ROMAN ALLIES								
Allied commander	Field Commander/Troop Commander					40/25		1
Troop name	Troop Type				Capabilities		Points per base	Bases per BG	Total bases
	Type	Armour	Quality	Training	Shooting	Close Combat			
Cavalry	Cavalry	Armoured	Average	Undrilled	-	Light Spear, Swordsmen	12	4	0–4
		Protected					9		
Legionaries:									
Hastati & Principes	Heavy Foot	Armoured	Average	Drilled	-	Impact Foot, Swordsmen	10	4–8	8–16
		Protected					8		
Triarii	Heavy Foot	Armoured	Superior	Drilled	-	Offensive Spearmen	13	2–4	1 per 4 Hastati & Principes
Leves or Velites	Light Foot	Unprotected	Average	Drilled	Javelins	Light Spear	4	4–8	1 per 2 Hastati & Principes
		Protected					5		
Upgrade veteran legions to:									
Hastati & Principes	Heavy Foot	Armoured	Superior	Drilled	-	Impact Foot, Skilled Swordsmen	14	4–8	0–16
		Protected					11		
Triarii	Heavy Foot	Armoured	Elite	Drilled	-	Offensive Spearmen	16	2–4	1 per 4 Hastati & Principes
Leves or Velites	Light Foot	Unprotected	Average	Drilled	Javelins	Light Spear	4	4–8	1 per 2 Hastati & Principes
		Protected					5		

LATE REPUBLICAN ROMAN

This list covers Roman armies from 105 to 25 BC – from the reforms of Marius until the reforms of Augustus. During this period Gaul, Cyrenaica, Egypt, Syria and additional swathes of Asia Minor were added to the empire. A series of buffer client kingdoms were left in the east between the directly ruled territories and the Parthian kingdom, whose horse archers and cataphracts had proved a successful counter to the otherwise all-conquering legions. A feature of this period, continued throughout the rest of Roman history, was a series of civil wars. These culminated in the victory of Octavian, great-nephew and adoptive heir of Julius Caesar. The Republic was replaced by the Principate, with Octavian becoming the first Roman emperor under the name of Augustus.

Roman Legionaries, by Richard Hook © Osprey Publishing Ltd. Taken from Men-at-Arms 121: Armies of the Carthaginian Wars 265 – 146 BC.

THE LEGIONS

After the reforms of Marius, legionaries were no longer divided into hastati, principes and triarii, but were uniformly equipped with oval shield,

Legionary

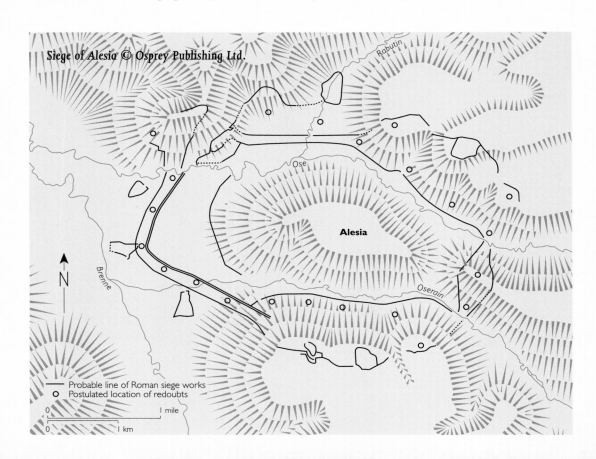

mail, pilum and sword. (As previously mentioned, the semi-cylindrical shield and lorica segmentata came into use later, in the 1st century AD). Maniples were replaced by larger tactical units called cohorts. Each legion had ten cohorts, each of 480 men at full strength. Later legions, though possibly not those of this period, had one larger senior cohort of 800 men.

The general quality of the legions was high, but some veteran legions became renowned for their prowess. Others on long-term postings in peaceful areas sometimes lost their edge.

AUXILIARY TROOPS

Cavalry and light troops were recruited from conquered and adjacent areas, but not yet organised into regular units. They included Spaniards, Gauls, Germans, Macedonians, Numidians, Thracians, Illyrians, Greeks, Syrians and others. Check out the lists for these nations to see which nations could provide which types.

Siege of Alesia © Osprey Publishing Ltd.

Robutin

Ose

Alesia

Brenne

Oserain

N

—— Probable line of Roman siege works
○ Postulated location of redoubts

0   1 mile
0   1 km

GAIUS JULIUS CAESAR (100 – 44 BC)

Roman politician, general and dictator. His conquest of Gaul started in 58 BC and culminated in the epic siege of Alesia in 52 BC. This conquest gave him much political kudos and a loyal veteran army.

Gaius Julius Caesar

During intervals in the fighting, he found time to invade Britain (abortively) twice in 55 and 54 BC. In 49 BC he made his bid for ultimate power, moving his army from Cisalpine Gaul into Roman Italy. This was against Roman law and triggered an epic civil war against the followers of Pompeius Magnus. After the final defeat of the Pompeian faction in 45 BC, Caesar returned to Rome glorious as Dictator for Life of the Roman Republic. However, on 15th March, 44 BC he was assassinated by a group of senatorial conspirators.

LATE REPUBLICAN ROMAN STARTER ARMY		
Commander-in-Chief	1	Inspired Commander (Caesar)
Sub-commanders	2	2 x Troop Commander
Legionaries	4 BGs	Each comprising 4 bases of legionaries: Superior, Armoured, Drilled Heavy Foot – Impact Foot, Skilled Swordsmen
Heavy cavalry	1 BG	4 bases of Gallic or German cavalry: Superior, Armoured, Undrilled Cavalry – Light Spear, Swordsmen
Light cavalry	2 BGs	Each comprising 4 bases of Numidian, Thracian or Illyrian light horse: Average, Unprotected, Undrilled Light Horse – Javelins, Light Spear
Illyrian foot	1 BG	8 bases of Illyrian foot: Average, Protected, Undrilled Medium Foot – Offensive Spearmen
Slingers	1 BG	6 bases of slingers: Average, Unprotected, Undrilled Light Foot – Sling
Camp	1	Fortified camp
Total	9 BGs	Camp, 12 mounted bases, 30 foot bases, 3 commanders

BUILDING A CUSTOMISED LIST USING OUR ARMY POINTS

Choose an army based on the maxima and minima in the list below. The following special instructions apply to this army:

- Commanders should be depicted as cavalry or legionaries.

- Thureophoroi can be graded as Medium Foot or Heavy Foot, but all must be graded the same.
- Only one allied contingent can be used.
- Gladiators cannot be used with any allies.
- Brutus and Cassius cannot use gladiators.

LATE REPUBLICAN ROMAN

Territory Types: Agricultural, Developed, Hilly, Woodland

C-in-C		Inspired Commander/Field Commander/Troop Commander				80/50/35		1
Sub-commanders		Field Commander				50		0–2
		Troop Commander				35		0–3

Troop name		Troop Type				Capabilities		Points per base	Bases per BG	Total bases
		Type	Armour	Quality	Training	Shooting	Close Combat			
Core Troops										
Legionaries		Heavy Foot	Armoured	Superior	Drilled	-	Impact Foot, Skilled Swordsmen	14	4–8	12–44
Upgrade veteran legionaries to		Heavy Foot	Armoured	Elite	Drilled	-	Impact Foot, Skilled Swordsmen	17	4–8	0–18
Downgrade slack legionaries to		Heavy Foot	Armoured	Average	Drilled	-	Impact Foot, Swordsmen	10	4–8	0–18
Downgrade raw legionaries to		Heavy Foot	Armoured	Poor	Drilled	-	Impact Foot, Swordsmen	8	4–8	0–18
Velites	Only before 80 BC	Light Foot	Unprotected	Average	Drilled	Javelins	Light Spear	4	6–8	0–12	6–20
			Protected					5			
Javelinmen		Light Foot	Unprotected	Average	Undrilled	Javelins	Light Spear	4		0–12	
Archers		Light Foot	Unprotected	Average	Undrilled	Bow	-	5		0–12	
Slingers		Light Foot	Unprotected	Average	Undrilled	Sling	-	4		0–12	
Heavy cavalry		Cavalry	Armoured	Superior	Undrilled	-	Light Spear, Swordsmen	16	4–6	4–8
			Protected	Superior				12		
			Armoured	Average				12		
			Protected	Average				9		
Light cavalry		Light Horse	Unprotected	Average	Undrilled	Javelins	Light Spear	7	4–6	0–8
Fortified camp								24		1
Optional Troops										
Cretan archers		Light Foot	Unprotected	Superior	Drilled	Bow	-	6	4–6	0–6
Spanish scutarii		Medium Foot	Protected	Average	Undrilled	-	Impact Foot, Swordsmen	7	6–8	0–12
Thracian foot		Medium Foot	Protected	Average	Undrilled	-	Heavy Weapon	7		
Illyrian or Rhaetian foot		Medium Foot	Protected	Average	Undrilled	-	Offensive Spearmen	7		
Ligurian foot		Medium Foot	Protected	Average	Undrilled	-	Light Spear	5		
Thureophoroi		All Medium Foot or all Heavy Foot	Protected	Average	Drilled	-	Offensive Spearmen	8		
Elephants		Elephants	-	Average	Undrilled	-	-	25	2	0–2
Gladiators		Medium Foot or Heavy Foot	Protected	Superior	Undrilled	-	Skilled Swordsmen	9	4	0–4
Bolt-shooters		Heavy artillery	-	Average	Drilled	Heavy Artillery	-	20	2	0–6
Syrian horse archers		Light Horse	Unprotected	Average	Undrilled	Bow	-	8	4	0–4
Field entrenchments		Field Fortifications						3		0–18
Allies										
Arab allies – Early Arab										
Armenian allies										
Bithynian allies										
Dacian allies – see Field of Glory Companion 5: Legions Triumphant: Imperial Rome At War.										
Galatian allies – see Field of Glory Companion 3: Immortal Fire: Greek, Persian and Macedonian Wars. (All foot must be imitation legionaries)										
Jewish allies – Later Jewish										
Numidian or Moorish allies										
Special Campaigns										
Brutus and Cassius in 42 BC										
Eastern or Thracian horse archers		Light Horse	Unprotected	Average	Undrilled	Bow	-	8	4–6	4–16
Eastern foot archers		Medium Foot	Unprotected	Average	Undrilled	Bow	-	5	6–8	0–8

LATE REPUBLICAN ROMAN ALLIES

Allied commander		Field Commander/Troop Commander					40/25	1	
Troop name		**Troop Type**				**Capabilities**	**Points per base**	**Bases per BG**	**Total bases**
		Type	Armour	Quality	Training	Shooting	Close Combat		

Troop name		Type	Armour	Quality	Training	Shooting	Close Combat	Points per base	Bases per BG	Total bases
Legionaries		Heavy Foot	Armoured	Superior	Drilled	-	Impact Foot, Skilled Swordsmen	14	4–8	4–12
Downgrade slack legionaries to		Heavy Foot	Armoured	Average	Drilled	-	Impact Foot, Swordsmen	10	4–8	All or none
Velites	Only before 80 BC	Light Foot	Unprotected	Average	Drilled	Javelins	Light Spear	4	4–6	0–6
			Protected					5		
Javelinmen		Light Foot	Unprotected	Average	Undrilled	Javelins	Light Spear	4		
Archers		Light Foot	Unprotected	Average	Undrilled	Bow	-	5		
Slingers		Light Foot	Unprotected	Average	Undrilled	Sling	-	4		
Heavy cavalry		Cavalry	Armoured	Superior	Undrilled	-	Light Spear, Swordsmen	16	4	0–4
			Protected	Superior				12		
			Armoured	Average				12		
			Protected	Average				9		
Light cavalry		Light Horse	Unprotected	Average	Undrilled	Javelins	Light Spear	7	4	

BITHYNIAN ALLIES

The small kingdom of Bithynia, in north-west Asia Minor, was an independent kingdom from 297 BC until 74 BC when the last king bequeathed his kingdom to Rome. The Bithynians were of Thracian origin. Bithynia allied with Rome against Mithridates VI of Pontus. Not much is known about the composition of Bithynian armies, so the following list is highly speculative.

- The commander should be depicted as cavalry.

BITHYNIAN ALLIES

Allied commander	Field Commander/Troop Commander						40/25	1	
Troop name	**Troop Type**				**Capabilities**		**Points per base**	**Bases per BG**	**Total bases**
	Type	Armour	Quality	Training	Shooting	Close Combat			

Troop name	Type	Armour	Quality	Training	Shooting	Close Combat	Points per base	Bases per BG	Total bases
Cavalry	Cavalry	Armoured	Superior	Undrilled	-	Light Spear, Swordsmen	16	4	0–4
				Drilled			17		
Light cavalry	Light Horse	Unprotected	Average	Undrilled	Javelins	Light Spear	7	4	
Citizen foot	Medium Foot or Heavy Foot	Protected	Average	Drilled	-	Offensive Spearmen	8	4	0–4
	Heavy Foot	Protected	Average	Drilled	-	Pikemen	6		
Peltasts	Medium Foot	Protected	Average	Undrilled	-	Light Spear	5	6–8	8–20
Javelinmen	Light Foot	Unprotected	Average	Undrilled	Javelins	Light Spear	4	4–6	0–6
Archers	Light Foot	Unprotected	Average	Undrilled	Bow	-	5	4	0–4

GALLIC

Gaesati Mercenary

This list covers Gallic armies from the beginning of the 4th century BC until 50 BC when Caesar's conquest was complete. Gauls mainly fought in close order, often with overlapping shields, and were disadvantaged in rough terrain, but some hill tribes probably fought in looser order in their familiar terrain. Gaesati were a Gallic warrior society. They fought naked, but with the usual Gallic shield and weapons. Large Gallic armies were usually coalitions of several tribes.

GAULS VS ROME

The history of the relationship between Gauls and Rome is one of conflict lasting centuries. In 387 BC the Senones under Brennus defeated the Roman army and sacked Rome itself. This trauma was forever to colour Roman relations with Gallic tribes. The Gauls in Northern Italy (Cisalpine Gaul) remained a danger, inflicting a number of defeats on the Romans until the Gallic defeat at Telamon in 225 BC. When Hannibal invaded Italy at the start of the Second Punic War seven years later the Gallic Boii and Insubres joined him and took part in his many victories over the Romans. In 121 BC, southern Gaul (Transalpine Gaul) was incorporated as a Roman province. In 58 BC, a mass migration by the Helvetii gave Julius Caesar the opportunity to commence his conquest of Gaul, culminating in the siege of Alesia in 52 BC, which represented the last effective defence of the Gauls, under Vercingetorix, against their age-old enemies. Contrary to the popular view of Gauls as "wild barbarians", their infantry usually advanced in good order in close formation, the advance culminating in a fierce massed charge. The bravest warriors, such as the Gaesati, often fought naked apart from their shields and weapons.

Vercingetorix. Caesar said of Vercingetorix "he terrorised waverers with the rigours of an iron discipline". © R Sheridan / AAA Collection Ltd.

GALLIC STARTER ARMY

Commander-in-Chief	1	Field Commander
Sub-commanders	2	2 x Troop Commander
Warriors	5 BGs	Each comprising 8 bases of warriors: Average, Protected, Undrilled Heavy Foot – Impact Foot, Swordsmen
Armoured cavalry	1 BG	4 bases of cavalry: Superior, Armoured, Undrilled Cavalry – Light Spear, Swordsmen
Cavalry	2 BGs	Each comprising 4 bases of cavalry: Superior, Protected, Undrilled Cavalry – Light Spear, Swordsmen
Javelinmen	1 BG	8 bases of javelinmen: Average, Unprotected, Undrilled Light Foot – Javelins, Light Spear
Camp	1	Unfortified camp
Total	9 BGs	Camp, 12 mounted bases, 48 foot bases, 3 commanders

BUILDING A CUSTOMISED LIST USING OUR ARMY POINTS

Choose an army based on the maxima and minima in the list below. The following special instructions apply to this army:

- Commanders should be depicted as chariots (only before 100 BC) or cavalry (only from 300 BC).

- Before 250 BC, excluding commanders' bases, chariot bases must at least equal cavalry bases, afterwards cavalry bases must at least equal chariot bases.

- Unless the C-in-C is of the same origin, troops only permitted to a certain origin can only be fielded under the command of an allied commander of that origin. All Gaesati must be under the command of one allied commander who can command only Gaesati. Other Gallic allied commanders' contingents must conform to the Gallic allies list below, but the troops in the contingent are deducted from the minima and maxima in the main list.

- Soldurii cannot be used with Gaesati, Germans or Ligurians.

- Only one non-Gallic allied contingent can be used.

- Plashed wood edge can only be used in plantations or forest.

Chariot

GALLIC

Territory Types: Agricultural, Woodlands

C-in-C	Inspired Commander/Field Commander/Troop Commander						80/50/35		1	
Sub-commanders	Field Commander/Troop Commander						50/35		0–2	
Gallic allied commanders	Field Commander/Troop Commander						40/25		0–2	

Troop name		Troop Type				Capabilities		Points per base	Bases per BG	Total bases	
		Type	Armour	Quality	Training	Shooting	Close Combat				
Core Troops											
Chariots	Only before 100 BC	Light Chariots	-	Superior	Undrilled	-	Light Spear	15	4–6	0–24	4–24
Cavalry	Only from 300 BC	Cavalry	Armoured	Superior	Undrilled	-	Light Spear, Swordsmen	16	4–6	0–6	
		Cavalry	Protected	Superior	Undrilled	-	Light Spear, Swordsmen	12	4–6	4–24	
Warriors	Only lowland tribes	Heavy Foot	Protected	Average	Undrilled	-	Impact Foot, Swordsmen	7	8–12	24–96	
	Only hill tribes	Medium Foot	Protected	Average	Undrilled	-	Impact Foot, Swordsmen	7	8–12		
Javelinmen		Light Foot	Unprotected	Average	Undrilled	-	Light Spear	4	6–8	6–8	
Optional Troops											
Soldurii		Heavy Foot	Armoured	Elite	Undrilled	-	Impact Foot, Swordsmen	15	4–6	0–6	
Gaesati mercenaries	Only before 200 BC	Heavy Foot	Protected	Superior	Undrilled	-	Impact Foot, Swordsmen	9	8–12	0–24	
Archers		Light Foot	Unprotected	Average	Undrilled	Bow	-	5	6–8	0–8	
Slingers		Light Foot	Unprotected	Average	Undrilled	Sling	-	4	6–8		
Families		Mob	Unprotected	Poor	Undrilled	-	-	2	8–12	0–12	
Wagon laager to protect flanks		Field Fortifications						3		0–12	
Plashed wood edge		Field Fortifications						3			
Fortified camp								24		0–1	
Allies											
Early German allies – See Field of Glory Companion 5: *Legions Triumphant: Imperial Rome At War.*											
Ligurian allies											
Spanish (Iberian) allies											

GALLIC ALLIES

Allied commander		Field Commander/Troop Commander						40/25		1	
Troop name		Troop Type				Capabilities		Points per base	Bases per BG	Total bases	
		Type	Armour	Quality	Training	Shooting	Close Combat				
Chariots	Only before 100 BC	Light Chariots	-	Superior	Undrilled	-	Light Spear	15	4–6	4–8	
Cavalry	Only from 300 BC	Cavalry	Protected	Superior	Undrilled	-	Light Spear, Swordsmen	12	4–6		
Warriors	Only lowland tribes	Heavy Foot	Protected	Average	Undrilled	-	Impact Foot, Swordsmen	7	8–12	8–24	
	Only hill tribes	Medium Foot	Protected	Average	Undrilled	-	Impact Foot, Swordsmen	7	8–12		
Javelinmen		Light Foot	Unprotected	Average	Undrilled	-	Light Spear	4	4	0–4	

LIGURIAN ALLIES

The Ligurian tribes by this period were confined to the hills of north-west Italy, having been displaced by the Gauls from the fertile lowlands. They sometimes fought as allies to the surrounding nations.

- The commander should be depicted as warriors.

LIGURIAN ALLIES								
Allied commander	Field Commander/Troop Commander						40/25	1
Troop name	Troop Type				Capabilities		Points per base	Bases per BG	Total bases
	Type	Armour	Quality	Training	Shooting	Close Combat			
Warriors	Medium Foot	Protected	Average	Undrilled	-	Light Spear	5	8–12	8–24
Javelinmen	Light Foot	Unprotected	Average	Undrilled	Javelins	Light Spear	4	4–6	0–6

Gallic warriors, 1st century BC, by Angus McBride. Taken from Men-at-Arms 158: Rome and her Enemies (2) Gallic and British Celts.

PYRRHIC

This list covers the army of Pyrrhos of Epiros from 280 to 272 BC: from his landing in Italy until his death. During this time he campaigned in Italy, Sicily and Greece with mixed success. Cavalry could be Epirot, Macedonian, Greek, Thessalian, Oscan, Acarnanian, Aitolian or Athamanian. Hoplites could be mercenaries, or supplied by allied Greek or Italiot states.

GENERAL PYRRHOS OF EPIROS (318 – 272 BC)

Named by Hannibal as the second greatest general of all time after Alexander the Great, Pyrrhos is famous for his "Pyrrhic victories" against the Romans in which, although he won, his armies suffered exceptionally heavy casualties. As he was the only Hellenistic general to defeat a major Roman army in battle, his victories can nevertheless be regarded as great achievements. He also campaigned against the Carthaginians in Sicily and against various rivals in Greece and Macedonia. He was killed in a street battle in Argos in 272 BC, after being stunned by a roof tile thrown by an old woman.

The Macedonian phalanx formation, from T. A. Dodge's Alexander.

THE MACEDONIAN PHALANX

Developed by King Philip II of Macedon in the 4th century BC, used by his son Alexander the Great to conquer the Persian empire and by Alexander's successors (including Pyrrhos), the Macedonian phalanx was the invincible infantry of its day. Armed with the 18ft (5.5m) pike (sarissa), the spear points of the first 5 ranks projected beyond the front rank, forming an impenetrable wall of spears. The commonest formation was 16 ranks deep, although other formations were used at times. In a straight ahead fight, in good terrain, the phalanx was supreme, but it could come unstuck in less favourable circumstances. The Roman victories against Hellenistic armies were mostly a result of the Romans exploiting their more flexible formations to catch the phalanx at a disadvantage. For example, at Kynoskephalai (197 BC) they charged the engaged phalanx in the rear, and at Corinth (146 BC) in the flank. At Pydna (168 BC) the phalanx was disordered by uneven ground. At Magnesia (190 BC) the phalanx was forced to remain static due to the threat of outflanking cavalry until assorted missiles hurled at the elephants in the intervals between the phalanx blocks drove the elephants to panic and break up the phalanx formation.

PYRRHIC STARTER ARMY

Commander-in-Chief	1	Inspired Commander (Pyrrhos)
Sub-commanders	2	2 x Troop Commander
Xystophoroi	1 BG	4 bases of xystophoroi: Superior, Armoured, Drilled Cavalry – Lancers, Swordsmen
Javelin-armed heavy cavalry	1 BG	4 bases of cavalry: Average, Armoured, Drilled Cavalry – Light Spear, Swordsmen
Tarantine light horse	1 BG	4 bases of light horse: Average, Unprotected, Drilled Light Horse – Javelins, Light Spear
Elephants	1 BG	2 bases of elephants: Average Elephants.
Phalanx	2 BGs	Each comprising 8 bases of phalangites: Average, Protected, Drilled Heavy Foot – Pikemen
Tarantine phalanx	1 BG	12 bases of phalangites: Poor, Protected, Drilled Heavy Foot – Pikemen
Samnite javelinmen	1 BG	8 bases of medium foot javelinmen: Average, Protected, Drilled Medium Foot – Light Spear, Swordsmen
Slingers	1 BG	6 bases of slingers: Average, Unprotected, Drilled Light Foot – Sling
Camp	1	Fortified camp
Total	9 BGs	Camp, 14 mounted bases, 42 foot bases, 3 commanders

Roman infantry fighting the Macedonian phalanx at the battle of Pydna, 168 BC, by Angus McBride. Taken from Men-at-Arms 291: Republican Roman Army 200–104 BC.

BUILDING A CUSTOMISED LIST USING OUR ARMY POINTS

Choose an army based on the maxima and minima in the list below. The following special instructions apply to this army:

- Commanders should be depicted as xystophoroi or javelin-armed heavy cavalry.

Javelin-Armed Heavy Cavalry

PYRRHIC										
Territory Types: Agricultural, Developed, Hilly										
C-in-C		Inspired Commander						80	1	
Sub-commanders		Field Commander						50	0–2	
		Troop Commander						35	0–3	
Troop name		Troop Type				Capabilities		Points per base	Bases per BG	Total bases
		Type	Armour	Quality	Training	Shooting	Close Combat			
Core Troops										
Xystophoroi	Only before 274 BC	Cavalry	Armoured	Superior	Drilled	-	Lancers, Swordsmen	17	4–6	4–6
Javelin-armed heavy cavalry	Before 274 BC	Cavalry	Armoured	Superior	Drilled	-	Light Spear, Swordsmen	17	4–6	4–6
				Average				13		
	From 274 BC	Cavalry	Armoured	Superior	Drilled	-	Light Spear, Swordsmen	17	4–6	6–12
				Average				13		
Light cavalry		Light Horse	Unprotected	Average	Undrilled or Drilled	Javelins	Light Spear	7	4–6	0–6
Phalanx		Heavy Foot	Protected	Average	Drilled	-	Pikemen	6	8–12	12–64
Hoplites		Heavy Foot	Protected	Average	Drilled	-	Offensive Spearmen	8	6–8	0–24
		Heavy Foot	Protected	Average	Undrilled	-	Offensive Spearmen	7		
				Poor				5		
Archers		Light Foot	Unprotected	Average	Drilled	Bow	-	5	6–8	0–12
Slingers		Light Foot	Unprotected	Average	Drilled	Sling	-	4	6–8	0–12	6–24
Javelinmen		Light Foot	Unprotected	Average	Undrilled	Javelins	Light Spear	4	6–8	0–12
Optional Troops										
Elephants		Elephants	Average	Undrilled	-	-	-	25	2	0–2
Fortified camp								24		0–1
Special Campaigns										
In Italy from 280 BC to 275 BC										
Downgrade phalanx as Tarentines		Heavy Foot	Protected	Poor	Drilled	-	Pikemen	4	8–12	8–32
Samnite, Lucanian or Bruttian javelinmen		Medium Foot	Protected	Average	Drilled	-	Light Spear, Swordsmen	7	6–8	6–24
In Greece from 274 BC to 273 BC										
Galatians		Heavy Foot	Protected	Superior	Undrilled	-	Impact Foot, Swordsmen	9	6–12	0–12

LATER CARTHAGINIAN

This list covers Carthaginian armies from 275 BC until 146 BC, from the aftermath of the war against Pyrrhos of Epiros until the Roman destruction of Carthage at the end of the Third Punic War.

At the start of the period, Carthage ruled a commercial empire in North Africa, Sicily, Sardinia, Corsica and southern Spain. After losing Sicily, Sardinia and Corsica to the Romans in and after the First Punic War, the Carthaginians concentrated on expanding their empire in Spain under the command of Hannibal's father Hamilcar Barca. After Hamilcar's death in 228 BC, his son-in-law Hasdrubal the Fair took command. He, however, was assassinated in 221 BC, following which Hannibal became command-in-chief. His siege and capture of Saguntum, a Roman ally in Spain, in 219 BC triggered the start of the Second Punic War.

GENERAL HANNIBAL (247 TO C.183 BC)

Carthaginian commander-in-chief and in large part instigator of the Second Punic War against Rome, Hannibal is famed as one of the greatest generals of all time. His march across the Alps in 218 BC to bring the war to the Romans at home is justly hailed as one of the outstanding feats of military history, though most of his elephants were so out of condition after the trek that they died after the Battle of Trebbia. He won victory after victory over the Roman armies whenever they were foolish enough to engage him in battle, the most famous being that of Cannae in 216 BC, but he never succeeded in capturing Rome itself. Eventually the Romans learned to avoid open battle and merely contain Hannibal in southern Italy. Meanwhile their armies conquered the Carthaginian possessions in Spain. Eventually they landed in North Africa and threatened Carthage itself. Hannibal was recalled, but was defeated by Scipio Africanus at the Battle of Zama in 202 BC. He died in exile circa 183 BC — committing suicide rather than be handed over to the Romans.

WAR ELEPHANTS

Used by the Hellenistic kingdoms, the Carthaginians and even the Romans, war elephants were a major feature of warfare in this period. They were feared by all troops, but were particularly effective against cavalry whose horses they terrified. As well as being hard to obtain and expensive to maintain, they were something of a risky weapon. Notable successes include defeating the Roman cavalry at Heraclea (280 BC), routing the Galatian cavalry and chariots at "the Elephant Victory" (273 BC), trampling the Roman legions at Bagradas (255 BC) and breaking the Macedonian left wing at Kynoskephalai (197 BC) and Pydna (168 BC). Notable disasters include panicking and disrupting their own cavalry at Zama (202 BC) and their own phalanx at Magnesia (190 BC).

THE END OF CARTHAGE

After defeat in the Second Punic War, Carthage lost all its possessions outside modern Tunisia, was forced to pay enormous reparations, and effectively reduced to the status of a Roman vassal. In 149 BC the Romans, using an unsuccessful punitive action by Carthage against Numidian raiders as a

Hannibal

BATTLE OF TREBBIA © Osprey Publishing Ltd

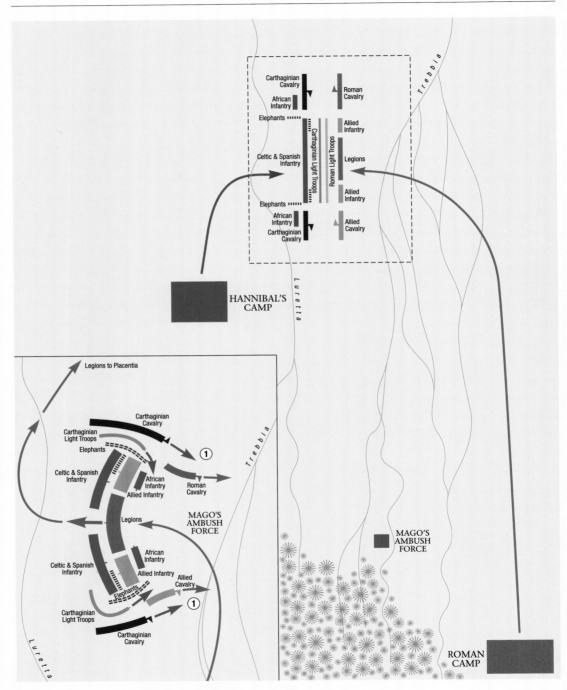

pretext, declared war on Carthage again, starting the 3rd Punic War. In 146 BC, Carthage itself was taken, following which the surviving citizens were sold into slavery, the city was razed to the ground and the surrounding fields sowed with salt.

African Veteran

LATER CARTHAGINIAN STARTER ARMY

Commander-in-Chief	1	Inspired Commander (Hannibal)
Sub-commanders	2	2 x Troop Commander
Gallic cavalry	1 BG	4 bases of cavalry: Superior, Protected, Undrilled Cavalry – Light Spear, Swordsmen
Spanish cavalry	1 BG	4 bases of cavalry: Superior, Protected, Undrilled Cavalry – Light Spear, Swordsmen
Numidian cavalry	2 BGs	Each comprising 4 bases of light horse: Average, Unprotected, Undrilled Light Horse – Javelins, Light Spear
Elephants	1 BG	2 bases of elephants: Average Elephants.
African spearmen	2 BGs	Each comprising 6 bases of spearmen: Average, Protected, Drilled Heavy Foot – Offensive Spearmen
Gallic warriors	1 BG	8 bases of warriors: Average, Protected, Undrilled Heavy Foot – Impact Foot, Swordsmen
Spanish scutarii	1 BG	6 bases of scutarii: Average, Protected, Undrilled Medium Foot – Impact Foot, Swordsmen
Numidian javelinmen	1 BG	6 bases of javelinmen: Average, Unprotected, Undrilled Light Foot – Javelins, Light Spear
Balearic slingers	1 BG	6 bases of slingers: Superior, Unprotected, Undrilled Light Foot – Sling
Camp	1	Unfortified camp
Total	11 BGs	Camp, 18 mounted bases, 38 foot bases, 3 commanders

BUILDING A CUSTOMISED LIST USING OUR ARMY POINTS

Choose an army based on the maxima and minima in the list below. The following special instructions apply to this army:

- Commanders should be depicted as Libyphoenician cavalry.
- Hannibal must be an Inspired Commander.

- Only Bruttian and Lucanian allies can be used together.
- From 200 BC, none of the following can be used: Spanish, Gallic, Celtiberian, Balearic, Ligurian, Campanian, Bruttian or Lucanian troops, Elephants nor any allies.
- Emergency levies cannot be used in mainland Italy.

LATER CARTHAGINIAN

Territory Types: Agricultural, Developed

C-in-C	Inspired Commander/Field Commander/Troop Commander					80/50/35	1	
Sub-commanders	Field Commander					50	0–2	
	Troop Commander					35	0–3	

Troop name	Troop Type				Capabilities		Points per base	Bases per BG	Total bases
	Type	Armour	Quality	Training	Shooting	Close Combat			
Core Troops									
Gallic or Spanish cavalry	Cavalry	Armoured	Superior	Undrilled	-	Light Spear, Swordsmen	16	4	0–4 / 4–12
	Cavalry	Protected	Superior	Undrilled	-	Light Spear, Swordsmen	12	4–6	0–12
Numidian or Spanish light cavalry	Light Horse	Unprotected	Average	Undrilled	Javelins	Light Spear	7	4–6	6–12
African spearmen	Heavy Foot	Protected	Average	Drilled	-	Offensive Spearmen	8	6–8	6–18
Numidian, Libyan, Moorish or Spanish javelinmen	Light Foot	Unprotected	Average	Undrilled	Javelins	Light Spear	4	6–8	6–16
Spanish mercenary scutarii	Medium Foot	Protected	Average	Undrilled	-	Impact Foot, Swordsmen	7	6–8	0–12
				Drilled			8		
Balearic slingers	Light Foot	Unprotected	Superior	Undrilled	Slings	-	5	4–6	0–6
Optional Troops									
Libyphoenician cavalry	Cavalry	Armoured	Superior	Drilled	-	Light Spear, Swordsmen	17	4	0–4
Poeni foot	Medium Foot	Protected	Average	Drilled	-	Light Spear, Swordsmen	7	6–8	0–8
Poeni or other emergency levies	Medium Foot	Protected	Poor	Drilled	-	Light Spear, Swordsmen	5	6–8	0–40
Gallic foot	All Heavy Foot or all Medium Foot	Protected	Average	Undrilled	-	Impact Foot, Swordsmen	7	8–12	0–24
Greek mercenary hoplites	Only before 235	Heavy Foot	Protected	Average	Drilled	-	Offensive Spearmen	8	6–8	0–16
Greek mercenary thureophoroi	Only before 235	Medium Foot or Heavy Foot	Protected	Average	Drilled	-	Offensive Spearmen	8	4–6	0–6
Celtiberian mercenary scutarii	Only from 235 to 201	Heavy Foot	Protected	Average	Undrilled	-	Impact Foot, Swordsmen	7	6–8	0–8
					Drilled	-		8	
Ligurian foot	Medium Foot	Protected	Average	Undrilled	-	Light Spear	5	6–8	0–12
Campanian hoplites	Heavy Foot	Protected	Average	Drilled	-	Offensive Spearmen	8	6–8	0–8
			Poor				6		
Campanian, Bruttian or Lucanian javelinmen	Medium Foot	Protected	Average	Drilled	-	Light Spear, Swordsmen	7	6–8	
			Poor				5		
Elephants	Elephants	-	Average	Undrilled	-	-	25	2	0–6
Bolt-shooters	Heavy Artillery	-	Average	Drilled	Heavy Artillery	-	20	2	0–2
Fortified camp							24		0–1
Allies									
Numidian allies									
Siceliot Greek allies (Only before 235 BC) – See Field of Companion 3: Immortal Fire: Greek, Persian and Macedonian Wars.									
Spanish allies									
Syracusan allies – See See Field of Companion 3: Immortal Fire: Greek, Persian and Macedonian Wars.									

Special Campaigns									
Hannibal in mainland Italy 216 BC to 203 BC									
Upgrade African spearmen to veterans with captured Roman equipment	Heavy Foot	Armoured	Superior	Drilled	-	Offensive Spearmen	13	6–8	All
Upgrade Gallic foot to	All Heavy Foot or all Medium Foot	Protected	Average	Drilled	-	Impact Foot, Swordsmen	8	6–8	All
Upgrade Campanian javelinmen and hoplites to Roman style foot	Heavy Foot	Armoured	Average	Drilled	-	Impact Foot, Swordsmen	10	4–8	All
		Protected	Average				8		
		Armoured	Poor				8		
		Protected	Poor				6		
Bruttian allies									
Lucanian allies									
Campanian allies – Late Campanian									
The following are not permitted: Artillery, more than 2 elephants, Celtiberian scutarii, undrilled Spanish scutarii, Syracusan, Numidian or Spanish allies.									
Hannibal in Africa 202 BC									
Upgrade African veteran spearmen to	Heavy Foot	Armoured	Superior	Drilled	-	Offensive Spearmen	13	6–8	6–8
Upgrade Bruttian veteran javelinmen to	Medium Foot	Armoured	Superior	Drilled	-	Light Spear, Swordsmen	12	6–8	6–8
Moorish archers	Light Foot	Unprotected	Average	Undrilled	Bow	-	5	4	0–4
The following are not permitted: Syracusan or Spanish allies.									

BRUTTIAN OR LUCANIAN ALLIES

The Bruttii and Lucani were Oscan peoples living in the far south-west of Italy. Their foot fought with javelins and swords.

- The commander should be depicted as cavalry.

BRUTTIAN OR LUCANIAN ALLIES								
Allied commander	Field Commander/Troop Commander						40/25	1
Troop name	Troop Type				Capabilities		Points per base	Bases per BG	Total bases
	Type	Armour	Quality	Training	Shooting	Close Combat			
Cavalry	Cavalry	Protected	Average	Undrilled	-	Light Spear, Swordsmen	9	4	0–4
Javelinmen	Medium Foot	Protected	Average	Drilled	-	Light Spear, Swordsmen	7	6–8	6–24
Skirmishers	Light Foot	Unprotected	Average	Undrilled	Javelins	Light Spear	4	6–8	0–8

LATE CAMPANIAN ALLIES

The Campani were an Oscan people who took over the Greek and Etruscan cities south of Latium in south-western Italy in the late 5th century BC. They were heavily influenced by Greek culture, fielding armies including both hoplites and Oscan-style javelinmen. This allied list only covers the period of the Second Punic War, however, by which time they had probably adopted Roman military equipment and organization.

- The commander should be depicted as cavalry.
- Hastati & Principes:Triarii:Skimishers quality must either be Average:Superior:Average, Average:Average:Average, Poor:Average:Poor or Poor:Poor:Poor.

LATE CAMPANIAN ALLIES

Allied commander	Field Commander/Troop Commander						40/25		1	
Troop name	Troop Type				Capabilities		Points per base	Bases per BG	Total bases	
	Type	Armour	Quality	Training	Shooting	Close Combat				
Cavalry	Cavalry	Protected	Superior	Undrilled	-	Light Spear, Swordsmen	12	4–6	0–6	
				Drilled			13			
Hastati & Principes	Heavy Foot	Protected	Average	Drilled	-	Impact Foot, Swordsmen	8	4–8	8–24	
			Poor				6			
Triarii	Heavy Foot	Protected	Superior	Drilled	-	Offensive Spearmen	10	2–4	1 per 4 Hastati & Principes	
			Average				8			
			Poor				6			
Skirmishers	Light Foot	Unprotected	Average	Undrilled	Javelins	Light Spear	4	4–8	0–8	
			Poor				2			

ILLYRIAN

Illyria occupied the area east of the Adriatic Sea and north-west of Greece. The Illyrian tribes were fond of raiding by land and sea for slaves and loot. Unlike most ancient peoples they armed their slaves, who fought alongside them in battle. This list covers Illyrian armies from the later 4th century BC until the beginning of the 1st century AD. Prior to this period they had used mainly skirmishing tactics, but now they fought in formed bodies of spearmen. Rome fought a series of wars against the Illyrians from 229 BC onwards, the last tribes being subjugated in 9 AD.

Slinger

ILLYRIAN STARTER ARMY

Commander-in-Chief	1	Field Commander
Sub-commanders	2	2 x Troop Commander
Cavalry	1 BG	6 bases of light horse: Average, Unprotected, Undrilled Light Horse – Javelins, Light Spear
Warriors	6 BGs	Each comprising 8 bases of warriors: Average, Protected, Undrilled Medium Foot – Offensive Spearmen
Javelinmen	2 BGs	Each comprising 6 bases of javelinmen: Average, Unprotected, Undrilled Light Foot – Javelins, Light Spear
Archers	1 BG	6 bases of archers: Average, Unprotected, Undrilled Light Foot – Bow
Slingers	1 BG	6 bases of slingers: Average, Unprotected, Undrilled Light Foot – Sling
Camp	1	Unfortified camp
Total	11 BGs	Camp, 6 mounted bases, 72 foot bases, 3 commanders

BUILDING A CUSTOMISED LIST USING OUR ARMY POINTS

Choose an army based on the maxima and minima in the list below. The following special instructions apply to this army:

- Commanders should be depicted as cavalry.

PAIONIAN ALLIES

The Paionian tribes, north of Macedon, used mainly skirmishing tactics.

- The commander should be depicted as cavalry or warriors.

ILLYRIAN

Territory Types: Hilly, Woodlands, Mountains

Troop name	Troop Type				Capabilities		Points per base	Bases per BG	Total bases
C-in-C	Inspired Commander/Field Commander/Troop Commander						80/50/35		1
Sub-commanders	Field Commander						50	0–2	
	Troop Commander						35	0–3	
	Type	Armour	Quality	Training	Shooting	Close Combat			
Core Troops									
Cavalry	Light Horse	Unprotected	Average	Undrilled	Javelins	Light Spear	7	4–6	0–6
Warriors	Medium Foot	Protected	Average	Undrilled	-	Offensive Spearmen	7	6–8	32–144
Javelinmen	Light Foot	Unprotected	Average	Undrilled	Javelins	Light Spear	4	6–8	6–16
Optional Troops									
Archers	Light Foot	Unprotected	Average	Undrilled	Bow	-	5	6–8	0–12
Slingers	Light Foot	Unprotected	Average	Undrilled	Sling	-	4	6–8	0–12
Allies									
Paionian allies									
Special Campaigns									
Against Epiros in 385 BC									
Illyrians equipped as hoplites	Heavy Foot	Protected	Average	Undrilled	-	Offensive Spearmen	7	6–8	0–8

Note: the Optional Troops Archers and Slingers share a combined maximum of 0–16.

Syracusan allies – See Field of Glory Companion 3: Immortal Fire: Greek, Persian, and Macedonian Wars.

PAIONIAN ALLIES

Troop name	Troop Type				Capabilities		Points per base	Bases per BG	Total bases
Allied commander	Field Commander/Troop Commander						40/25		1
	Type	Armour	Quality	Training	Shooting	Close Combat			
Cavalry	Light Horse	Unprotected	Average	Undrilled	Javelins	Light Spear	7	4	0–4
Warriors	Light Foot	Unprotected	Average	Undrilled	Javelins	Light Spear	4	6–8	12–36
	Medium Foot	Protected	Average	Undrilled	-	Light Spear	5	6–8	
Slingers	Light Foot	Unprotected	Average	Undrilled	Sling	-	4	4	0–4
Archers	Light Foot	Unprotected	Average	Undrilled	Bow	-	5	4	
Levies	Light Foot	Unprotected	Poor	Undrilled	Javelins	Light Spear	2	6–8	0–12
	Medium Foot	Protected	Poor	Undrilled	-	Light Spear	3	6–8	

ANCIENT SPANISH

This list covers the tribes of the Iberian peninsula from the mid-3rd century BC until the last rebellions were crushed by the Romans at the end of the 1st century BC. There were three main tribal groupings – Iberians, Lusitanians and Celtiberians.

SPANISH SCUTARII & CAETRATI

Called scutarii by the Romans because of their large oval shield (*scutum*), Spanish (Iberian) foot were much sought after as mercenaries or allies by the Carthaginians and Romans. Armed with heavy javelins and sword, their charge was fierce and hard to resist. They were undisciplined when victorious but resolute in defeat, often making desperate suicidal charges or even committing mass suicide rather than surrender when besieged. They were famous for their mobility over the craggy wooded hills of Spain. They were fond of ambushes and all forms of guerrilla warfare – the Roman pacification of Spain was a long and painful process. Their skirmishers were called *caetrati* by the Romans after their smaller round shield (*caetra*).

Celtiberian scutarii were similarly equipped to Iberians, but less adept in rough and broken terrain. Lusitanian foot were all caetrati rather than scutarii, but a proportion at least were equipped for close combat, some even wearing mail.

Lusitanian

IBERIAN STARTER ARMY		
Commander-in-Chief	1	Field Commander
Sub-commanders	2	2 x Troop Commander
Large shield cavalry	1 BG	4 bases of cavalry: Superior, Protected, Undrilled Cavalry – Light Spear, Swordsmen
Small shield cavalry	2 BGs	Each comprising 4 bases of light horse: Average, Unprotected, Undrilled Light Horse – Javelins, Light Spear
Celtiberian mercenary scutarii	2 BGs	Each comprising 8 bases of Celtiberian scutarii: Average, Protected, Undrilled Heavy Foot – Impact Foot, Swordsmen
Iberian scutarii	3 BGs	Each comprising 8 bases of Iberian scutarii: Average, Protected, Undrilled Medium Foot – Impact Foot, Swordsmen
Caetrati	2 BGs	Each comprising 8 bases of javelinmen: Average, Unprotected, Undrilled Light Foot – Javelins, Light Spear
Slingers	1 BG	8 bases of slingers: Average, Unprotected, Undrilled Light Foot – Sling
Camp	1	Unfortified camp
Total	11 BGs	Camp, 12 mounted bases, 64 foot bases, 3 commanders

Hispanic Warriors, 2nd century BC, by Angus McBride. Taken from Men-at-Arms 180: Rome's Enemies (4) Spanish Armies.

BUILDING A CUSTOMISED LIST USING OUR ARMY POINTS

Choose an army based on the maxima and minima in the list below. The following special instructions apply to this army:

- Commanders should be depicted as large shield cavalry.
- Unless the C-in-C is of the same origin, troops only permitted to a certain origin can only be fielded under the command of an allied commander of that origin. A Spanish allied commander's contingent must conform to the Ancient Spanish allies list below, but the troops in the contingent are deducted from the minima and maxima in the main list.

Scutarius

31

ANCIENT SPANISH

Territory Types: Agricultural, Hilly

							Points per base	Bases per BG	Total bases
C-in-C	Inspired Commander/Field Commander/Troop Commander						80/50/35		1
Sub-commanders	Field Commander/Troop Commander						50/35		0–2
Spanish allied commanders	Field Commander/Troop Commander						40/25		0–2

Troop name	Troop Type				Capabilities		Points per base	Bases per BG	Total bases
	Type	Armour	Quality	Training	Shooting	Close Combat			
Core Troops									
Large shield cavalry	Cavalry	Protected	Superior	Undrilled	-	Light Spear, Swordsmen	12	4–6	0–6
Small shield cavalry	Light Horse	Unprotected	Average	Undrilled	Javelins	Light Spear	7	4–6	0–12
Caetrati	Light Foot	Unprotected	Average	Undrilled	Javelins	Light Spear	4	6–8	12–110
Iberians only									
Scutarii	Medium Foot	Protected	Average	Undrilled	-	Impact Foot, Swordsmen	7	6–12	24–96
Lusitanians only									
Heavy caetrati	Medium Foot	Protected	Average	Undrilled	-	Impact Foot, Swordsmen	7	6–12	16–48
Celtiberians only									
Scutarii	Heavy Foot	Protected	Average	Undrilled	-	Impact Foot, Swordsmen	7	6–12	28–120
Optional Troops									
Slingers	Light Foot	Unprotected	Average	Undrilled	Sling	-	4	6–8	0–12
Iberians or Lusitanians only									
Mercenary Celtiberians	Heavy Foot	Protected	Average	Undrilled	-	Impact Foot, Swordsmen	7	6–12	0–24
Special Campaigns									
Sertorius's Lusitanians – 80 BC to 72 BC									
Upgrade Sertorius to Inspired Commander									1
Upgrade large shield cavalry to	Cavalry	Protected	Superior	Drilled	-	Light Spear, Swordsmen	13	4	Any
Upgrade heavy caetratri to	Medium Foot	Protected	Average	Drilled	-	Impact Foot, Swordsmen	8	4–6	Any
Legionaries	Heavy Foot	Armoured	Superior	Drilled	-	Impact Foot, Skilled Swordsmen	14	4–8	0–8

ANCIENT SPANISH ALLIES

							Points per base	Bases per BG	Total bases
Allied commander	Field Commander/Troop Commander						40/25		1

Troop name	Troop Type				Capabilities		Points per base	Bases per BG	Total bases
	Type	Armour	Quality	Training	Shooting	Close Combat			
Small shield cavalry	Light Horse	Unprotected	Average	Undrilled	Javelins	Light Spear	7	4	0–4
Caetrati	Light Foot	Unprotected	Average	Undrilled	Javelins	Light Spear	4	6–8	6–24
Iberians only									
Scutarii	Medium Foot	Protected	Average	Undrilled	–	Impact Foot, Swordsmen	7	6–12	6–24
Lusitanians only									
Heavy caetrati	Medium Foot	Protected	Average	Undrilled	–	Impact Foot, Swordsmen	7	6–12	6–12
Celtiberians only									
Scutarii	Heavy Foot	Protected	Average	Undrilled	–	Impact Foot, Swordsmen	7	6–12	8–32

Iberian Warriors, 2nd century BC, by Angus McBride.
Taken from Men-at-Arms 180: Rome's Enemies
(4) Spanish Armies.

LATER MACEDONIAN

Cretan Archer

Following the death of Alexander the Great, Macedon, north of Greece, was one of the three main kingdoms into which Alexander's empire was divided after the initial round of civil wars between his successors. (The others were the Seleucid kingdom in the east, and the Ptolemaic kingdom in Egypt). This list covers the armies of the Kingdom of Macedon from about 260 BC. Until the advent of Rome, the Kingdom of Macedon was the dominant force in Greece. Between 215 and 148 BC, Macedon fought a series of wars against the expanding Roman Republic. After the fourth Macedonian war, in 148 BC, Macedon was annexed by Rome.

LATER MACEDONIAN STARTER ARMY		
Commander-in-Chief	1	Field Commander
Sub-commanders	2	2 x Troop Commander
Macedonian & Thessalian cavalry	2 BGs	Each comprising 4 bases of cavalry: Superior, Armoured, Drilled Cavalry – Light Spear, Swordsmen
Illyrian cavalry	1 BG	4 bases of light horse: Average, Unprotected, Undrilled Light Horse – Javelins, Light Spear
Agema	1 BG	8 bases of Agema pikemen: Superior, Protected, Drilled Heavy Foot – Pikemen
Chalkaspides and Leukaspides	2 BGs	Each comprising 8 bases of pikemen: Average, Protected, Drilled Heavy Foot – Pikemen
Thureophoroi	1 BG	6 bases of thureophoroi: Average, Protected, Drilled Medium Foot – Offensive Spearmen
Illyrian foot	1 BG	6 bases of Illyrian foot: Average, Protected, Undrilled Medium Foot – Offensive Spearmen
Javelinmen	1 BG	6 bases of javelinmen: Average, Unprotected, Undrilled Light Foot – Javelins, Light Spear
Cretan archers	1 BG	6 bases of archers: Superior, Unprotected, Drilled Light Foot – Bow
Camp	1	Unfortified camp
Total	10 BGs	Camp, 12 mounted bases, 48 foot bases, 3 commanders

BUILDING A CUSTOMISED LIST USING OUR ARMY POINTS

Choose an army based on the maxima and minima in the list below. The following special instructions apply to this army:

- Commanders should be depicted as heavy cavalry.
- Thureophoroi and thorakitai can be graded as Medium Foot or Heavy Foot, but all of both types must be graded the same.

LATER MACEDONIAN

Territory Types: Agricultural, Developed, Hilly

C-in-C	Inspired Commander/Field Commander/Troop Commander						80/50/35	1	
Sub-commanders	Field Commander						50	0–2	
	Troop Commander						35	0–3	

Troop name	Troop Type				Capabilities		Points per base	Bases per BG	Total bases
	Type	Armour	Quality	Training	Shooting	Close Combat			
Core Troops									
Macedonian, Greek or Thessalian heavy cavalry	Cavalry	Armoured	Superior	Drilled	–	Light Spear, Swordsmen	17	4–6	4–12
			Average				13		
Thracian or Galatian heavy cavalry	Cavalry	Armoured	Superior	Undrilled	–	Light Spear, Swordsmen	16	4–6	0–6
			Average				12		
Illyrian, Thracian or Greek light cavalry	Light Horse	Unprotected	Average	Undrilled	Javelins	Light Spear	7	4–6	0–6
Agema and "peltasts"	Heavy Foot	Protected	Superior	Drilled	–	Pikemen	8	8–12	8–24
Chalkaspides and Leukaspides	Heavy Foot	Protected	Average	Drilled	–	Pikemen	6	8–12	12–56
Thureophoroi	All Medium Foot or all Heavy Foot	Protected	Average	Drilled	–	Offensive Spearmen	8	6–8	6–18
Javelinmen	Light Foot	Unprotected	Average	Drilled or Undrilled	Javelins	Light Spear	4	6–8	0–16 / 6–28
Cretans	Light Foot	Unprotected	Superior	Drilled	Bow	–	6	6–8	0–12
Optional Troops									
Upgrade thureophoroi to thorakitai	Medium Foot or Heavy Foot	Armoured	Average	Drilled	–	Offensive Spearmen	10	6–8	0–8
Illyrians	Medium Foot	Protected	Average	Undrilled	–	Offensive Spearmen	7	6–8	0–16
Thracians	Medium Foot	Protected	Average	Undrilled	–	Heavy weapon	7	6–8	
Galatians	Heavy Foot	Protected	Superior	Undrilled	–	Impact Foot, Swordsmen	9	6–8	0–8
			Average				7		
Bolt-shooters	Heavy artillery	–	Average	Drilled	Heavy Artillery	–	20	2	0–2
Fortified camp							24		0–1
Allies									
Achaian allies – Hellenistic Greek – See Field of Glory Companion 3: *Immortal Fire: Greek, Persian and Macedonian Wars*									

ATTALID PERGAMENE

The Attalid dynasty began with Philetaeros (son of Attalos), Lysimachos' governor of the great city of Pergamon in western Asia Minor. He switched sides to Seleukos in 282 BC. His nephew and successor, Eumenes I, declared independence in 262 BC. This list covers Pergamene armies from that date. Pergamon was allied with Rome against Macedon in the First, Second and Third Macedonian wars, and against the Seleucid kingdom in the Syrian war. After the Roman and Pergamene victory over the Seleucids at Magnesia in 190 BC, Eumenes II was granted all the Seleucid territories west of the Taurus. The kingdom was bequeathed to Rome by Attalos III on his death in 133 BC. His illegitimate half brother, Aristonikos, rebelled but was suppressed by 129 BC.

Galatian Cavalry

ATTALID PERGAMENE STARTER ARMY		
Commander-in-Chief	1	Field Commander
Sub-commanders	2	2 x Troop Commander
Xystophoroi	1 BG	4 bases of xystophoroi: Superior, Armoured, Drilled Cavalry – Lancers, Swordsmen
Galatian cavalry	1 BG	4 bases of Galatian cavalry: Superior, Armoured, Undrilled Cavalry – Light Spear, Swordsmen
Light cavalry	1 BG	4 bases of light horse: Average, Unprotected, Undrilled Light Horse – Javelins, Light Spear
Thureophoroi	3 BGs	Each comprising 6 bases of thureophoroi: Average, Protected, Drilled Medium Foot – Offensive Spearmen
Galatian foot	2 BGs	Each comprising 6 bases of Galatian foot: Superior, Protected, Undrilled Heavy Foot – Impact Foot, Swordsmen
Cretan archers	1 BG	6 bases of Cretan archers: Superior, Unprotected, Drilled Light Foot – Bow
Trallian slingers	1 BG	8 bases of Trallian slingers: Average, Unprotected, Undrilled Light Foot – Sling
Camp	1	Unfortified camp
Total	10 BGs	Camp, 12 mounted bases, 44 foot bases, 3 commanders

BUILDING A CUSTOMISED LIST USING OUR ARMY POINTS

Choose an army based on the maxima and minima in the list below. The following special instructions apply to this army:

- Commanders should be depicted as xystophoroi.
- Thureophoroi can be graded as Medium Foot or Heavy Foot, but all must be graded the same.

ATTALID PERGAMENE

Territory Types: Agricultural, Developed, Hilly

C-in-C	Inspired Commander/Field Commander/Troop Commander						80/50/35	1	
Sub-commanders	Field Commander						50	0–2	
	Troop Commander						35	0–3	

Troop name	Troop Type				Capabilities		Points per base	Bases per BG	Total bases
	Type	Armour	Quality	Training	Shooting	Close Combat			
Core Troops									
Xystophoroi	Cavalry	Armoured	Superior	Drilled	–	Lancers, Swordsmen	17	4–6	4–8
			Average				13		
Galatian cavalry	Cavalry	Armoured	Superior	Undrilled	–	Light Spear, Swordsmen	16	4	0–4
Light cavalry	Light Horse	Unprotected	Average	Undrilled	Javelins	Light Spear	7	4–6	0–6
Thureophoroi	All Medium Foot or all Heavy Foot	Protected	Average	Drilled	–	Offensive Spearmen	8	6–8	12–48
Traditional peltasts	Light Foot	Unprotected	Average	Drilled	Javelins	Light Spear	4	6–8	
Cretan archers	Light Foot	Unprotected	Superior	Drilled	Bow	–	6	6–8	6–12
Trallian slingers	Light Foot	Unprotected	Average	Undrilled	Sling	–	4	6–8	6–8
Optional Troops									
Citizen militia	Medium Foot or Heavy Foot	Protected	Poor	Drilled	–	Offensive Spearmen	6	6–8	0–12
Galatian foot	Heavy Foot	Protected	Superior	Undrilled	–	Impact Foot, Swordsmen	9	6–12	0–16
			Average				7		
Mysian or other javelinmen	Medium Foot	Protected	Average	Undrilled	–	Light Spear	5	6–8	0–36
	Light Foot	Unprotected	Average	Undrilled	Javelins	Light Spear	4	6–8	
Cataphracts (Only after 190 BC)	Cataphracts	Heavily Armoured	Average	Drilled	–	Lancers, Swordsmen	16	4	0–4
Phalangites (Only after 190 BC)	Heavy Foot	Protected	Average	Drilled	–	Pikemen	6	8–12	0–12
Elephants (Only after 190 BC)	Elephants	–	Average	Undrilled	–	–	25	2	0–2
Bolt shooters or stone throwers	Heavy Artillery	–	Average	Drilled	Heavy Artillery	–	20	2	0–4
Fortified camp							24		0–1
Allies									
Kappadokian allies									
Special Campaigns									
Only Attalos I in 218 BC									
Galatian allies – see Field of Glory Companion 3: *Immortal Fire: Greek, Persian and Macedonian Wars*									

ATTALID PERGAMENE ALLIES								
Allied commander	Field Commander/Troop Commander					40/25	1	
Troop name	Troop Type				Capabilities		Points per base	Bases per BG	Total bases
	Type	Armour	Quality	Training	Shooting	Close Combat			
Xystophoroi	Cavalry	Armoured	Superior	Drilled	–	Lancers, Swordsmen	17	4	4
			Average				13		
Galatian cavalry	Cavalry	Armoured	Superior	Undrilled	–	Light Spear, Swordsmen	16	4	0–4
Light cavalry	Light Horse	Unprotected	Average	Undrilled	Javelins	Light Spear	7	4	
Thureophoroi	All Medium Foot or all Heavy Foot	Protected	Average	Drilled	–	Offensive Spearmen	8	4–8	4–12
Traditional peltasts	Light Foot	Unprotected	Average	Drilled	Javelins	Light Spear	4	4–8	
Cretan archers	Light Foot	Unprotected	Superior	Drilled	Bow	–	6	4	0–4
Trallian slingers	Light Foot	Unprotected	Average	Undrilled	Sling	–	4	4	0–4

KAPPADOKIAN ALLIES

The small kingdom of Kappadokia in eastern Asia Minor existed from 330 BC to 17 AD, with a brief occupation by Alexander's successors from 322 to 301 BC. It sometimes provided allied contingents to the surrounding states.

• The commander should be depicted as cavalry.

KAPPADOKIAN ALLIES								
Allied commander	Field Commander/Troop Commander					40/25	1	
Troop name	Troop Type				Capabilities		Points per base	Bases per BG	Total bases
	Type	Armour	Quality	Training	Shooting	Close Combat			
Cavalry	Cavalry	Armoured	Superior	Undrilled	-	Light Spear, Swordsmen	16	4–6	4–6
Light cavalry	Light Horse	Unprotected	Average	Undrilled	Javelins	Light Spear	7	4–6	4–6
Javelinmen	Medium Foot	Protected	Average	Undrilled	-	Light Spear	5	6–8	6–18
Archers	Light Foot	Unprotected	Average	Undrilled	Bow	-	5	4–8	4–8
	Medium Foot	Unprotected	Average	Undrilled	Bow	-	5	4–8	

NUMIDIAN OR EARLY MOORISH

The ancient Numidians and Moors were semi-nomadic Berber tribes living in North West Africa. The Numidian kingdom was west of Carthage and the Moorish kingdom beyond that. This list covers Numidian and early Moorish armies from the late 3rd century BC to the early 1st century AD.

Numidian and Moorish cavalry and foot fought mainly as javelin skirmishers, in which role they were expert, harassing the enemy with javelins but using superior speed and agility to evade their charges. The Carthaginians made much use of Numidian cavalry and foot during the Punic Wars against Rome. At the Battle of Cannae in 216 BC, the Numidian cavalry on the Carthaginian right wing skirmished with the opposing Roman cavalry and kept them out of the battle long

Numidian Warrior, by Richard Hook. Taken from Men-at-Arms 121: Armies of the Carthaginian Wars 261 – 146 BC.

enough for the Spanish and Gallic cavalry on the Carthaginian left to be able to defeat the Roman cavalry facing them, ride round the Roman rear, and attack the cavalry of the other Roman wing before falling on the rear of the Roman infantry. They were fond of ambushes and other tricks, and made excellent use of terrain. They were at their best in pursuit of fleeing enemy, but when put to flight themselves would flee for two or three days before risking stopping.

Under the influence of the Romans, various attempts were made to develop drilled close fighting foot. King Juba I of Numidia was allied to the Pompeian side in the Roman Civil War. Bogud (Bogus) of Mauretania was allied to Caesar.

Numidian Cavalry

NUMIDIAN STARTER ARMY

Commander-in-Chief	1	Field Commander (Juba I)
Sub-commanders	2	2 x Troop Commander
Gallic & Spanish bodyguard	1 BG	4 bases of Gallic and Spanish cavalry: Superior, Protected, Undrilled Cavalry – Light Spear, Swordsmen
Cavalry	3 BGs	Each comprising 6 bases of Numidian cavalry: Average, Unprotected, Undrilled Light Horse – Javelins, Light Spear
Javelinmen	2 BGs	Each comprising 8 bases of Numidian foot javelinmen: Average, Unprotected, Undrilled Light Foot – Javelins, Light Spear
Imitation legionaries	4 BGs	Each comprising 6 bases of imitation legionaries: Average, Protected, Drilled Heavy Foot – Impact Foot, Swordsmen
Elephants	1 BG	2 bases of elephants: Average, Undrilled Elephants
Camp	1	Unfortified camp
Total	11 BGs	Camp, 24 mounted bases, 40 foot bases, 3 commanders

BUILDING A CUSTOMISED LIST USING OUR ARMY POINTS

Choose an army based on the maxima and minima in the list below. The following special instructions apply to this army:

- Commanders should be depicted as cavalry or Gallic & Spanish bodyguard.

NUMIDIAN OR EARLY MOORISH

Territory Types: Agricultural, Hilly, Steppes

C-in-C	Inspired Commander/Field Commander/Troop Commander						80/50/35	1	
Sub-commanders	Field Commander						50	0–2	
	Troop Commander						35	0–3	

Troop name	Troop Type				Capabilities		Points per base	Bases per BG	Total bases
	Type	Armour	Quality	Training	Shooting	Close Combat			
Core Troops									
Cavalry	Light Horse	Unprotected	Average	Undrilled	Javelins	Light Spear	7	4–6	16–72
Javelinmen	Light Foot	Unprotected	Average	Undrilled	Javelins	Light Spear	4	6–8	16–96
Optional Troops									
Archers	Light Foot	Unprotected	Average	Undrilled	Bow	-	5	6–8	0–12
Slingers	Light Foot	Unprotected	Average	Undrilled	Sling	-	4	6–8	
Elephants	Elephants	-	Average	Undrilled	-	-	25	2	0–4
Close fighting foot	Medium Foot	Protected	Average	Drilled	-	Light Spear	6	6–8	0–24
			Poor				4		
Imitation Legionaries	Only from 55 BC	Heavy Foot	Protected	Average	Drilled	-	Impact Foot, Swordsmen	8	4–8	
				Poor				6		
Special Campaigns									
Juba I from 55 BC to 46 BC									
Gallic & Spanish bodyguard	Cavalry	Protected	Superior	Undrilled	-	Light Spear, Swordsmen	12	4	0–4
Bogus in 47 BC									
Spanish foot	Medium Foot	Protected	Average	Undrilled	-	Impact Foot, Swordsmen	7	6–8	0–8
Juba II from 3 AD to 6 AD									
Roman allies – Principate Roman – see Field of Glory Companion 5: *Legions Triumphant: Imperial Rome At War*.									

NUMIDIAN OR EARLY MOORISH ALLIES

Allied commander		Field Commander/Troop Commander						40/25		1	
Troop name		Troop Type				Capabilities		Points per base	Bases per BG	Total bases	
		Type	Armour	Quality	Training	Shooting	Close Combat				
Cavalry		Light Horse	Unprotected	Average	Undrilled	Javelins	Light Spear	7	4–6	4–18	
Javelinmen		Light Foot	Unprotected	Average	Undrilled	Javelins	Light Spear	4	4–8	4–24	
Close fighting foot		Medium Foot	Protected	Average	Drilled	-	Light Spear	6	6–8	0–12	
				Poor				4			
Imitation Legionaries	Only from 55 BC	Heavy Foot	Protected	Average	Drilled	-	Impact Foot, Swordsmen	8	4–8		
				Poor				6			
Elephants		Elephants	-	Average	Undrilled	-	-	25	2	0–2	

LATER SELEUCID

The Seleucid Kingdom was the largest in land area of the Hellenistic Successor kingdoms that formed after the death of Alexander the Great. At its height it stretched from the eastern shores of the Aegean Sea to India. This list covers Seleucid armies from 205 BC. At this stage, the kingdom still reached from western Asia Minor to India, but had lost Bactria in the north-east to local Greek rebels. About this time, the Seleucid cavalry were upgraded to fully armoured cataphracts – probably following Antiochos III's eastern campaigns against the Graeco-Bactrian kingdom. In 192 BC, he invaded Greece, but was defeated by the Romans at Thermopylae in 191 BC and again at Magnesia in Asia Minor in 190 BC. Following these defeats, the kingdom lost most of Asia Minor. Soon after, the Parthians,

Armoured Elephant

under King Mithridates I (170–138 BC), took over most of the eastern Seleucid provinces, leaving only Syria and Mesopotamia. Constant civil wars took further toll, and in 63 BC, the Romans deposed the last Seleucid princes and made the remnants of the kingdom into a Roman province.

SCYTHED CHARIOTS AT MAGNESIA

Bristling with razor-sharp blades, scythed chariots were designed to strike fear into the hearts of the enemy. When successful, their effect could be devastating. Appian describes the result of a Pontic scythed chariot charge at the Battle of the River Amnias in 88 BC: "The scythed chariots were driven at great speed against the Bithynians, cutting some of them in two instantaneously, and tearing others to pieces. The army of Nicomedes was terrified at seeing men cut in halves and still breathing, or mangled in fragments, or hanging on the scythes. Overcome rather by the hideousness of the spectacle than by loss of the fight, fear disordered their ranks."

However, scythed chariots were fairly easy to counter with light foot archers, slingers and javelinmen, who could shoot at the horses while dodging out of the way of the chariots. This happened at the Battle of Magnesia. The Seleucid chariot horses, maddened by their wounds, stampeded through their own cataphracts and camelry. The Pergamene cavalry (allied to the Romans) following closely behind were able to sweep away the Seleucid wing and threaten the flank of the phalanx. Unable to safely advance, the phalanx had to stand under a hail of missiles from the Roman foot until the elephants in the intervals between the phalanx blocks panicked and broke up the phalanx, completing the Seleucid defeat.

LATER SELEUCID STARTER ARMY		
Commander-in-Chief	1	Troop Commander
Sub-commanders	2	2 x Troop Commander
Cataphracts	2 BGs	Each comprising 4 bases of cataphracts: Superior, Heavily Armoured, Drilled Cataphracts – Lancers, Swordsmen
Horse archers	1 BG	4 bases of horse archers: Average, Unprotected, Undrilled Light Horse – Bow
Elephants	1 BG	2 bases of elephants: Average Elephants
Argyraspides	1 BG	8 bases of Argyraspides pikemen: Superior, Protected, Drilled Heavy Foot – Pikemen
Phalanx	2 BGs	Each comprising 8 bases of pikemen: Average, Protected, Drilled Heavy Foot – Pikemen
Thureophoroi	1 BG	6 bases of thureophoroi: Average, Protected, Drilled Medium Foot – Offensive Spearmen
Archers	1 BG	8 bases of archers: Poor, Unprotected, Undrilled Light Foot – Bow
Slingers	1 BG	8 bases of slingers: Poor, Unprotected, Undrilled Light Foot – Sling
Camp	1	Unfortified camp
Total	10 BGs	Camp, 14 mounted bases, 46 foot bases, 3 commanders

BUILDING A CUSTOMISED LIST USING OUR ARMY POINTS

Choose an army based on the maxima and minima in the list below. The following special instructions apply to this army:

- Commanders should be depicted as Companions or Agema.

- Only one allied contingent can be used.
- Aitolians cannot be used with post-166 BC options.
- Elymaian, Parthian or Jewish allies cannot be used with pre-166 BC options.
- Thureophoroi and thorakitai can be graded as Medium Foot or Heavy Foot, but all of both types must be graded the same.

LATER SELEUCID

Territory Types: Agricultural, Developed, Hilly								
C-in-C	Inspired Commander/Field Commander/Troop Commander					80/50/35	1	
Sub-commanders	Field Commander					50	0–2	
	Troop Commander					35	0–3	

Troop name	Troop Type				Capabilities		Points per base	Bases per BG	Total bases
	Type	Quality	Training	Armour	Shooting	Close Combat			
Core Troops									
Companions	Cavalry	Armoured	Elite	Drilled	–	Lancers, Swordsmen	20	2–4	0–4 / 4–12
Agema or other cataphracts	Cataphracts	Heavily Armoured	Superior	Drilled	–	Lancers, Swordsmen	20	4–6	4–12 / 4–12
			Average				16		
Argyraspides / Before 166 BC	Heavy Foot	Protected	Superior	Drilled	–	Pikemen	8	8–12	0–16
Argyraspides / From 166 BC	Heavy Foot	Protected	Superior	Drilled	–	Pikemen	8	8	0–8
	Heavy Foot	Armoured	Superior	Drilled	–	Impact Foot, Skilled Swordsmen	14	4–8	0–8
Phalanx	Heavy Foot	Protected	Average	Drilled	–	Pikemen	6	8–12	8–32
Thureophoroi	Medium Foot or Heavy Foot	Protected	Average	Drilled	–	Offensive Spearmen	8	4–6	0–6
Thorakitai	Medium Foot or Heavy Foot	Armoured	Average	Drilled	–	Offensive Spearmen	10	4–6	0–6
Archers	Light Foot	Unprotected	Average	Undrilled	Bow	–	5	6–8	0–16 / 6–24
			Poor				3		
Archers	Medium Foot	Unprotected	Average	Undrilled	Bow	–	5	6–8	0–16 / 6–24
			Poor				3		
Slingers	Light Foot	Unprotected	Average	Undrilled	Sling	–	4	6–8	0–16
			Poor				2		
Optional Troops									
Skythian cavalry	Light Horse or Cavalry	Unprotected	Average	Undrilled	Bow	Swordsmen	10	4	0–4
Other horse archers	Light Horse	Unprotected	Average	Undrilled	Bow	–	8	4	0–4
Cretan archers	Light Foot	Unprotected	Superior	Drilled	Bow	–	6	4–6	0–6
Javelinmen	Light Foot	Unprotected	Average	Undrilled or Drilled	Javelins	Light Spear	4	6–8	0–8
Hillmen	Medium Foot	Protected	Average	Undrilled	–	Light Spear	5	4–6	0–6
Thracians	Medium Foot	Protected	Average	Undrilled	–	Heavy Weapon	7	4–6	0–6
Tarantine cavalry	Light Horse	Unprotected	Average	Drilled	Javelins	Light Spear	7	4–6	0–6
Civic militia cavalry	Light Horse	Unprotected	Poor	Drilled	Javelins	Light Spear	5	4–6	0–6
Elephants / Only before 124 BC	Elephants	–	Average	Undrilled	–	–	25	2	0–4
Scythed chariots	Scythed Chariots	–	Average	Undrilled	–	–	15	2–4	0–4
Galatian cavalry	Cavalry	Armoured	Superior	Undrilled	–	Light Spear, Swordsmen	16	4	0–4
Galatian foot	Heavy Foot	Protected	Superior	Undrilled	–	Impact Foot, Swordsmen	9	4–6	0–6
			Average				7		
Arab camelry	Camelry	Unprotected	Poor	Undrilled	Bow	Swordsmen	10	4	0–4
Civic militia thureophoroi / Only from 166 BC	All Medium Foot or all Heavy Foot	Protected	Poor	Drilled	–	Offensive Spearmen	6	6–8	0–16
Massed levies	Mob	Unprotected	Poor	Undrilled	–	–	2	8–12	0–12
Bolt-shooters	Heavy Artillery	–	Average	Drilled	Heavy Artillery	–	20	2	0–2
Fortified camp							24		0–1

Allies
Aitolian allies – Hellenistic Greek – See Field of Glory Companion 3: *Immortal Fire: Greek, Persian and Macedonian Wars*
Elymaian allies
Jewish allies – Later Jewish
Parthian (rebel) allies

LATER PTOLEMAIC

The Ptolemaic kingdom in Egypt was one of the three major Hellenistic kingdoms into which Alexander the Great's empire was divided after the initial wars of his successors. (The others being Macedon, north of Greece, and the Seleucid kingdom in the east). As well as Egypt, the early Ptolemies used their substantial fleet to control much of the eastern Mediterranean coast. By 166 BC, when this list starts, their territories had been reduced to Egypt and Cyprus. About this time, a reorganisation of the army has been postulated in which infantry drilled in Roman legionary tactics were introduced. The list ends with the annexation of the kingdom by Rome in 30 BC after the defeat and death of Marcus Antonius and Cleopatra.

CLEOPATRA VII (69 – 30 BC)

Cleopatra VII was the last Ptolemaic ruler of Egypt, at various times as co-ruler with her father Ptolemy XII Auletes (until 51 BC), and her brothers/husbands Ptolemy XIII (from 51–47 BC) and Ptolemy XIV (from 47–44 BC). The Macedonian Ptolemaic dynasty, descended from Alexander the Great's general Ptolemy, continued the Pharaonic Egyptian tradition of brother-sister marriages. From 48 BC Cleopatra was in a state of civil war with her 14-year-old brother/husband Ptolemy XIII. This coincided with the defeat of Pompey by Julius Caesar in the Roman civil war. Pompey fled to Egypt, but was murdered by Ptolemy in the hope of gaining Caesar's good will. Caesar, however, sided with Cleopatra, restored her to power, and became her lover. Ptolemy was drowned while crossing the Nile. Cleopatra then married her 12-year-old younger brother Ptolemy XIV as co-ruler, though she retained the real power and continued her liaison with Caesar. She bore him a son, his only known male issue, known popularly as Caesarion (little Caesar). In 44 BC, after the death of Ptolemy XIV – probably poisoned by Cleopatra – Caesarion was appointed co-ruler at the age of 3 as Ptolemy XV Philopator Philometor Caesar. After Caesar's assassination, Cleopatra became the lover of Marcus Antonius (Mark Anthony) and bore him three children. When he fell out with Octavian, Caesar's heir, Cleopatra supported him in the ensuing civil war. Their fleet was defeated at Actium in 31 BC. They fled back to Egypt, where they committed suicide in 30 BC. Caesarion was captured by Octavian and murdered as a threat to his claim to be Julius Caesar's sole heir. Egypt became a Roman province. Despite the legend of Cleopatra's great beauty, Cleopatra's coins indicate that she was, in fact, rather plain. Contemporary writers admire her intelligence, charisma and seductive voice, but tactfully omit mention of her looks.

The Phalanx

LATER PTOLEMAIC STARTER ARMY

Commander-in-Chief	1	Field Commander
Sub-commanders	2	2 x Troop Commander
Xystophoroi	2 BGs	Each comprising 4 bases of xystophoroi: Average, Armoured, Drilled Cavalry – Lancers, Swordsmen
Light cavalry	1 BG	4 bases of light horse: Average, Unprotected, Drilled Light Horse – Javelins, Light Spear
Macedonian phalangites	3 BGs	Each comprising 8 bases of phalangites: Average, Protected, Drilled Heavy Foot – Pikemen
Romanised infantry	2 BGs	Each comprising 6 bases of Romanised infantry: Average, Armoured, Drilled Heavy Foot – Impact Foot, Swordsmen
Elephants	1 BG	2 bases of elephants: Average, Undrilled Elephants
Slingers	1 BG	8 bases of slingers: Average, Unprotected, Undrilled Light Foot – Sling
Camp	1	Unfortified camp
Total	10 BGs	Camp, 14 mounted bases, 44 foot bases, 3 commanders

BUILDING A CUSTOMISED LIST USING OUR ARMY POINTS

Choose an army based on the maxima and minima in the list below. The following special instructions apply to this army:

- Commanders should be depicted as xystophoroi.
- Thureophoroi and thorakitai can be graded as Medium Foot or Heavy Foot, but all of both types must be graded the same.

LATER PTOLEMAIC

Territory Types: Agricultural, Developed

C-in-C		Inspired Commander/Field Commander/Troop Commander					80/50/35	1	
Sub-commanders		Field Commander					50	0–2	
		Troop Commander					35	0–3	

Troop name		Troop Type				Capabilities		Points per base	Bases per BG	Total bases
		Type	Armour	Quality	Training	Shooting	Close Combat			
Core Troops										
Xystophoroi		Cavalry	Armoured	Superior	Drilled	–	Lancers, Swordsmen	17	4–6	4–8
				Average				13		
Light cavalry		Light Horse	Unprotected	Average	Drilled	Javelins	Light Spear	7	4	0–4
Guard phalangites	Before 55 BC	Heavy Foot	Protected	Superior	Drilled	–	Pikemen	8	8	0–8
Macedonian phalangites	Before 55 BC	Heavy Foot	Protected	Average	Drilled	–	Pikemen	6	8–12	24–48
Egyptian phalangites	Before 55 BC	Heavy Foot	Protected	Poor	Drilled	–	Pikemen	4	8–12	0–32
Phalangites	From 55 BC	Heavy Foot	Protected	Average	Drilled	–	Pikemen	6	8–12	0–16
				Poor				4		
Thureophoroi		All Medium Foot or all Heavy Foot	Protected	Average	Drilled	–	Offensive Spearmen	8	6–8	0–12
Thorakitai		All Medium Foot or all Heavy Foot	Armoured	Average	Drilled	–	Offensive Spearmen	10	6–8	
Romanised infantry		Heavy Foot	Protected	Average	Drilled	–	Impact Foot, Swordsmen	8	4–8	
			Armoured					10		
Archers		Light Foot	Unprotected	Average	Drilled	Bow	–	5	6–8	0–8
Slingers		Light Foot	Unprotected	Average	Drilled	Sling	–	4	6–8	0–8	0–16
Javelinmen		Light Foot	Unprotected	Average	Undrilled	Javelins	Light Spear	4	6–8	0–8
Optional Troops										
Greek mercenary cavalry		Cavalry	Armoured	Average	Drilled	–	Light Spear, Swordsmen	13	4	0–4
Galatian mercenary cavalry		Cavalry	Armoured	Superior	Undrilled	–	Light Spear, Swordsmen	16	4	
Nubian mercenary cavalry		Cavalry	Protected	Average	Undrilled	–	Light Spear, Swordsmen	9	4	
Thracians		Medium Foot	Protected	Average	Undrilled	–	Heavy weapon	7	4–6	0–6
Galatian foot	Only before 55 BC	Heavy Foot	Protected	Superior	Undrilled	–	Impact Foot, Swordsmen	9	4–6	0–6
				Average				7		
Cretan archers		Light Foot	Unprotected	Superior	Drilled	Bow	–	6	6–8	0–8
Cretan troops		Medium Foot	Protected	Poor	Drilled	–	Light Spear	4	6–8	0–8
Arab camelry		Camelry	Unprotected	Poor	Undrilled	Bow	Swordsmen	10	4	0–4
Elephants	Only before 55 BC	Elephants	–	Average	Undrilled	–	–	25	2	0–4
Roman legionaries	Only from 55 BC	Heavy Foot	Armoured	Superior	Drilled	–	Impact Foot, Skilled Swordsmen	14	4–8	0–12
		Heavy Foot	Armoured	Average	Drilled	–	Impact Foot, Swordsmen	10	4–8	
Bolt-shooters		Heavy Artillery	–	Average	Drilled	Heavy Artillery	–	20	2	0–4
Fortified camp								24		0–1

PONTIC

This list covers Pontic armies from 110 BC to 47 BC: The reigns of Mithridates the Great (Mithridates VI Eupator) and his son Pharnaces II.

MITHRIDATES VI (THE GREAT) OF PONTUS (132 – 63 BC)

Mithridates the Great of Pontus was one of the expanding Roman empire's most formidable and persistent foes. Starting with the small Kingdom of Pontus on the south coast of the Black Sea, he conquered the Kingdom of Bosporus on the north coast and expanded his borders in Anatolia at the expense of the neighbouring kingdoms. When these called on Rome for help, Mithridates' forces defeated the armies sent against him in 88 BC by the local Roman commander Manius Aquilius and the King of Bithynia, and surged on into Greece where they were welcomed by many cities, including Athens. Manius Aquilius was captured and molten gold

Sarmatian armoured lancer and horse-archer, by Gerry Embleton © Osprey Publishing Ltd. Taken from Men-at-Arms 373: The Sarmatians 600 BC – AD 450.

was poured down his throat as a fitting punishment for his notorius greed. This marked the apogee of Mithridates' success. A new Roman army, under the famous general Sulla, was sent to Greece and defeated the Pontic armies. Mithridates sued for peace. He then converted his army from a pike phalanx-based Hellenistic army to Roman style legions. Over the next 25 years, Mithridates fought two more wars against the Romans, sometimes successful, more

often defeated. Never one to give up hope, he ultimately fled to the Bosporus, where he started to raise a new army. This was too much for his long-suffering subjects, however, who finally revolted. Mithridates committed suicide with the help of a loyal soldier's sword – after famously taking antidotes throughout his life, he proved immune to self-administered poison.

After Mithridates' death his son Pharnaces II ruled in Bosporus. Seizing the opportunity presented by the Roman Civil War, he re-invaded Pontus, defeating the local Roman forces. However, when Caesar arrived in 47 BC he swiftly defeated Pharnaces at Zela. So short was the campaign that Caesar uttered his famous dictum "veni, vidi, vici" (I came, I saw, I conquered). Pharnaces fled back to the Bosporus but was soon deposed.

Scythed Chariot

PONTIC STARTER ARMY		
Commander-in-Chief	1	Field Commander
Sub-commanders	2	2 x Troop Commander
Pontic heavy cavalry	1 BG	6 bases of cavalry: Superior, Armoured, Undrilled Cavalry – Light Spear, Swordsmen
Pontic light cavalry	1 BG	4 bases of light horse: Average, Unprotected, Undrilled Light Horse – Javelins, Light Spear
Sarmatian cavalry	1 BG	4 bases of Sarmatian cavalry: Superior, Armoured, Undrilled Cavalry – Lancers, Swordsmen
Imitation legionaries	3 BGs	Each comprising 6 bases of imitation legionaries: Average, Protected, Drilled Heavy Foot – Impact Foot, Swordsmen
Thureophoroi	1 BG	6 bases of thureophoroi: Average, Protected, Drilled Medium Foot – Offensive Spearmen
Bastarnae	1 BG	6 bases of Bastarnae: Superior, Unprotected, Undrilled Medium Foot – Heavy Weapon
Javelinmen	1 BG	6 bases of javelinmen: Average, Unprotected, Undrilled Light Foot – Javelins, Light Spear
Archers	1 BG	6 bases of archers: Average, Unprotected, Undrilled Light Foot – Bow
Camp	1	Unfortified camp
Total	10 BGs	Camp, 14 mounted bases, 42 foot bases, 3 commanders

BUILDING A CUSTOMISED LIST USING OUR ARMY POINTS

Choose an army based on the maxima and minima in the list below. The following special instructions apply to this army:

- Commanders should be depicted as heavy cavalry.

- Mithridates cannot be an inspired commander. However, some of the generals to whom he delegated his conquests might qualify.
- Thureophoroi can be graded as Medium Foot or Heavy Foot, but all must be graded the same.

PONTIC

Territory Types: Agricultural, Developed, Hilly

Troop name		Troop Type				Capabilities		Points per base	Bases per BG	Total bases
C-in-C		Inspired Commander/Field Commander/Troop Commander						80/50/35		1
Sub-commanders		Field Commander						50	0–2	
		Troop Commander						35	0–3	
		Type	Armour	Quality	Training	Shooting	Close Combat			
Core Troops										
Heavy cavalry		Cavalry	Armoured	Superior	Undrilled	—	Light Spear, Swordsmen	16	4–6	4–8
Light cavalry		Light Horse	Unprotected	Average	Undrilled	Javelins	Light Spear	7	4–6	4–8
Javelinmen		Medium Foot	Protected	Average	Undrilled	—	Light Spear	5	6–8	6–32
		Light Foot	Unprotected	Average	Undrilled	Javelins	Light Spear	4	6–8	
Archers		Light Foot	Unprotected	Average	Undrilled	Bow	—	5	6–8	6–16
		Medium Foot	Unprotected	Average	Undrilled	Bow	—	5	6–8	
Thureophoroi		All Medium Foot or all Heavy Foot	Protected	Average	Drilled	—	Offensive Spearmen	8	6–8	6–18
Optional Troops										
Scythed chariots		Scythed Chariots	—	Average	Undrilled	—	—	15	2–4	0–4
Pikemen	Only before 84 BC	Heavy Foot	Protected	Average	Drilled	—	Pikemen	6	8–12	0–24
				Poor				4		
Imitation Legionaries	Before 84 BC	Heavy Foot	Protected	Average	Drilled	—	Impact Foot, Swordsmen	8	4–8	0–8
				Poor				6		
	From 84 BC	Heavy Foot	Protected	Average	Drilled	—	Impact Foot, Swordsmen	8	4–8	8–24
				Poor				6		
Sarmatian cavalry		Cavalry	Armoured	Superior	Undrilled	—	Lancers, Swordsmen	16	4–6	0–6
			Protected					12		
		Cavalry	Protected	Superior	Undrilled	Bow*	Light Spear, Swordsmen	14	4–6	
Skythian cavalry		Light Horse or Cavalry	Unprotected	Average	Undrilled	Bow	Swordsmen	10	4–6	0–6
Thracians		Medium Foot	Protected	Average	Undrilled	—	Heavy weapon	7	6–8	0–8
Bastarnae		Medium Foot	Unprotected	Superior	Undrilled	—	Heavy weapon	7	6–8	
Slingers		Light Foot	Unprotected	Average	Undrilled	Sling	—	4	4–6	0–6
Galatians		Heavy Foot	Protected	Average	Undrilled	—	Impact Foot, Swordsmen	7	6–8	0–8
Chalybes		Medium Foot	Unprotected	Average	Undrilled	—	Defensive Spearmen	5	4–6	0–6
Field fortifications		Field Fortifications						3		0–10
Fortified camp								24		0–1
Allies										
Armenian allies										

49

SPARTACUS SLAVE REVOLT

This list covers the slave armies of the Third Servile War.

In 73 BC, Spartacus was one of 70 gladiators who broke out of the school of Lentulus Batiatus in Capua. The rebels initially used kitchen implements to break out but obtained several carts of gladiatorial equipment during their escape. They then defeated a small force sent to recapture them, taking their arms and armour to add to their arsenal. Over the next few weeks, the rebels moved to a more defensible position on the slopes of Mount Vesuvius and many more escaped slaves swelled their ranks. A larger Roman militia force besieged the slaves but by using vines and ladders some of the slave force made its way down the impassable slopes and attacked the Roman camp from the rear. The resulting battle saw the Romans comprehensively defeated.

The army of Spartacus continued to grow and defeated yet another Roman force under Publius Varinius. By the end of 73 BC, the total size of the slave army was 70,000 men, women and children. In 72 BC, the slaves moved north and their still growing force split into at least two. The smaller portion, led by Crixus, was caught and defeated by a regular Roman army under Lucius Gellius Publicola.

Spartacus, however, was by now rather too near Rome for the comfort of the Senate. Several more hastily raised legions were sent to bar Spartacus' route to Rome while Gellius moved to trap the slave army. Spartacus then split his army, a small force kept the main Roman force busy while he turned on and defeated Gellius before returning with his whole force to defeat the blocking force as well.

At this point Spartacus declined to attack Rome and instead headed back to the south with his total force now numbering 120,000 or more. The following year, with the revolt now recognised as a serious issue, a force of eight legions under Marcus Licinius Crassus was sent after the slaves. The slave army was trapped in the toe of Italy. Crassus sent two of his legions under Mummius to try to get behind Spartacus with orders not to engage. Seeing an opportunity for glory Mummius disobeyed and attacked, only to be defeated. Crassus then attacked with his main force and for the first time the main slave army was beaten with several thousand casualties.

Spartacus then tried to find ways to escape by sea to Sicily but was unable to do so. The slaves retreated towards Rhegium, in the toe of Italy, followed by Crassus whose legions built a line of fortifications across the isthmus to pen the slaves in. With further veteran Roman troops under Pompey approaching, the slaves made a desperate break out but were caught by Crassus' legions and defeated in detail in two further battles. Spartacus is believed to have died fighting. 5,000 fleeing slaves were caught by Pompey and slaughtered, the 6,000 slaves captured by Crassus were crucified along the road between Capua and Rome.

Cavalryman

*Slaves sent to become gladiators by Angus McBride © Osprey Publishing Ltd. Taken from Warrior 39:
Gladiators 100 BC – AD 200.*

SLAVE REVOLT STARTER ARMY

Commander-in-Chief	1	Inspired Commander (Spartacus)
Sub-commanders	2	2 x Troop Commander
Cavalry	1 BG	4 bases of cavalry: Average, Protected, Undrilled Cavalry – Light Spear, Swordsmen
Gladiators with captured Roman armour and equipment	1 BG	8 bases of gladiators: Superior, Armoured, Undrilled Heavy Foot – Impact Foot, Skilled Swordsmen
Other slaves with captured Roman armour and equipment	2 BGs	Each comprising 6 bases of slaves: Average, Armoured, Undrilled Heavy Foot – Impact Foot, Swordsmen
Other slaves with captured Roman equipment	2 BGs	Each comprising 6 bases of slaves: Average, Protected, Undrilled Heavy Foot – Impact Foot, Swordsmen
Poorly equipped masses	2 BGs	Each comprising 10 bases of slaves: Average, Unprotected, Undrilled Mob – Light Spear
Javelinmen	1 BG	8 bases of javelinmen: Poor, Unprotected, Undrilled Light Foot – Javelins, Light Spear
Slingers	1 BG	8 bases of slingers: Poor, Unprotected, Undrilled Light Foot – Sling
Camp	1	Unfortified camp
Total	10 BGs	Camp, 4 mounted bases, 68 foot bases, 3 commanders

BUILDING A CUSTOMISED LIST USING OUR ARMY POINTS

Choose an army based on the maxima and minima in the list below. The following special instructions apply to this army:

- Commanders should be depicted as cavalry or gladiators.
- Slaves equipped with Roman weapons and armour can be graded as Heavy Foot or Medium Foot but must all be graded the same.

SPARTACUS SLAVE REVOLT
Territory Types: Agricultural, Developed, Hilly, Woodland

Troop name	Troop Type				Capabilities		Points per base	Bases per BG	Total bases
C-in-C	Inspired Commander/Field Commander/Troop Commander						80/50/35		1
Sub-commanders	Field Commander						50	0–2	
	Troop Commander						35	0–3	
	Type	Armour	Quality	Training	Shooting	Close Combat			
Core Troops									
Poorly equipped masses	Mob	Unprotected	Average	Undrilled	–	Light Spear	4	8–12	20–104
Slaves equipped with Roman weapons and armour	All Heavy Foot or All Medium Foot	Protected	Average	Undrilled	–	Impact Foot, Swordsmen	7	6–8	12–64 / 20–64
		Armoured	Average	Undrilled	–	Impact Foot, Swordsmen	9	6–8	0–24
Gladiators	Medium Foot or Heavy Foot	Protected	Superior	Undrilled	–	Skilled swordsmen	9	4	0–8
Gladiators with captured Roman arms & armour	Heavy Foot	Armoured	Superior	Undrilled	–	Impact Foot, Skilled swordsmen	13	4–8	
Javelinmen	Light Foot	Unprotected	Poor	Undrilled	Javelins	Light Spear	2	6–8	6–18
Optional Troops									
Slingers	Light Foot	Unprotected	Poor	Undrilled	Sling	–	2	6–8	0–8
Cavalry	Cavalry	Protected	Average	Undrilled	–	Light Spear, Swordsmen	9	4	0–4
Women, children and old men	Mob	Unprotected	Poor	Undrilled	–	–	2	8–12	0–24

EARLY ARMENIAN

The mountains of Armenia allowed the kingdom to maintain its independence from the great empires throughout this period. This list covers Armenian armies from the declaration of independence by Ervand (Orontes) II of the House of Ervand in 331 BC until the overthrow of Trdat II by the Sassanids in 252 AD.

TIGRAN THE GREAT (RULED 95 BC – 55BC)

During the reign of Tigran the Great, Armenia filled a power vacuum left by the weakening of the Parthian kingdom by nomad invasions and the collapse of the Seleucids, gaining a short-lived empire including Mesopotamia, Syria and Media-Atropatene. Allied with Mithridates VI of Pontus, whose daughter, Cleopatra, he married, Tigran allowed Mithridates to seek refuge in Armenia after his defeat by the Romans under Lucullus in 70 BC. The Romans demanded that Mithridates be handed over to them. Tigran refused. The following year Lucullus invaded. He defeated the Armenian army twice, at Tigranocerta and Artaxata, but failed to capture Tigran or Mithridates and was recalled. Mithridates returned to Pontus with 8,000 men. In 66 BC, with a new Roman army under Pompey the Great advancing into Armenia, Tigran capitulated. He was forced to give up his empire, but was allowed to keep his original kingdom, and ruled it as a Roman client until his death in 55 BC at the age of 85.

EARLY ARMENIAN STARTER ARMY		
Commander-in-Chief	1	Field Commander
Sub-commanders	2	2 x Troop Commander
Cataphracts	3 BGs	Each comprising 4 bases of cataphracts: Superior, Heavily Armoured, Undrilled Cataphracts – Lancers, Swordsmen
Horse archers	3 BGs	Each comprising 6 bases of light horse: Average, Unprotected, Undrilled Light Horse – Bow
Javelinmen	2 BGs	Each comprising 6 bases of javelinmen: Average, Protected, Undrilled Medium Foot – Light Spear
Archers	2 BGs	Each comprising 6 bases of archers: Average, Unprotected, Undrilled Light Foot – Bow
Camp	1	Unfortified camp
Total	10 BGs	Camp, 30 mounted bases, 24 foot bases, 3 commanders

BUILDING A CUSTOMISED LIST USING OUR ARMY POINTS

Choose an army based on the maxima and minima in the list below. The following special instructions apply to this army:

- Commanders should be depicted as cataphracts.
- An inspired commander cannot be used in Tigran the Great's reign.

Cataphract

EARLY ARMENIAN

Territory Types: Agricultural, Mountains

C-in-C	Inspired Commander/Field Commander/Troop Commander				80/50/35		1	
Sub-commanders	Field Commander				50		0–2	
	Troop Commander				35		0–3	

Troop name	Troop Type				Capabilities		Points per base	Bases per BG	Total bases
	Type	Armour	Quality	Training	Shooting	Close Combat			
Core Troops									
Cataphracts	Cataphracts	Heavily Armoured	Superior	Undrilled	–	Lancers, Swordsmen	18	4–6	4–18
Horse archers	Light Horse	Unprotected	Average	Undrilled	Bow	–	8	4–6	12–32
Javelinmen	Medium Foot	Protected	Average	Undrilled	–	Light Spear	5	6–8	6–72
Archers	Light Foot	Unprotected	Average	Undrilled	Bow	–	5	6–8	8–36
	Medium Foot	Unprotected	Average	Undrilled	Bow	–	5	6–8	
Optional Troops									
Slingers	Light Foot	Unprotected	Average	Undrilled	Sling	–	4	4–6	0–6
Servants	Mob	Unprotected	Poor	Undrilled	–	–	2	6–8	0–8
Fortified camp							24		0–1
Special Campaigns									
Tigran the Great from 83 BC to 69 BC									
Pikemen	Heavy Foot	Protected	Average	Drilled	–	Pikemen	6	8–12	0–12
			Poor				4		
Imitation Legionaries	Heavy Foot	Protected	Average	Drilled	–	Impact Foot, Swordsmen	8	4–8	0–12
			Poor				6		
Arab allies – Early Arab									
Media Atropatene allies									
Khosrov I's anti-Sassanid coalition from 226 AD to 228 AD									
Alan allies – see Field of Glory Companion 5: *Legions Triumphant: Imperial Rome At War*.									
Kushan or Parthian allies – use Parthian allies list									
Roman allies – Principate Roman – see Field of Glory Companion 5: *Legions Triumphant: Imperial Rome At War*.									

EARLY ARMENIAN

Parthian and Armenian cataphracts, by Angus McBride © Osprey Publishing Ltd. Taken from Men-at-Arms 175: Rome's Enemies (3) Parthians and Sassanid Persians.

EARLY ARMENIAN ALLIES

Allied commander	Field Commander/Troop Commander						40/25	1	
Troop name	**Troop Type**				**Capabilities**		**Points per base**	**Bases per BG**	**Total bases**
	Type	Armour	Quality	Training	Shooting	Close Combat			
Cataphracts	Cataphracts	Heavily Armoured	Superior	Undrilled	–	Lancers, Swordsmen	18	4–6	4–6
Horse archers	Light Horse	Unprotected	Average	Undrilled	Bow	–	8	4–6	4–12
Javelinmen	Medium Foot	Protected	Average	Undrilled	–	Light Spear	5	6–8	0–18
Archers	Light Foot	Unprotected	Average	Undrilled	Bow	–	5	6–8	0–12
	Medium Foot	Unprotected	Average	Undrilled	Bow	–	5	6–8	

PARTHIAN

The Parthian Kingdom at its height covered the whole of modern Iran as well as parts of the surrounding regions. Founded in the pre-existing province of Parthia south-east of the Caspian sea circa 250 BC by the nomadic Parni, the kingdom was ruled by the Arsacid dynasty. Parthia expanded east, south and west, taking over the eastern provinces of the Hellenistic Seleucid Kingdom. Eventually it came into conflict with the expanding Roman empire. The Parthians successfully halted Roman expansion in the east, their combination of light horse archers and heavily armoured cataphracts proving more than a match for the legions. The two empires continued as uneasy neighbours until the Parthian kingdom was overthrown by its Sassanid Persian vassals in 225 AD.

This list covers the Parthian kingdom from its foundation until its overthrow by the Sassanids. It also covers the Suren secessionist state in the east. Adiabene, Edessa, Elymais, Hatra and Media-Atropatene were vassal states.

THE BATTLE OF CARRHAE 53 BC

In this epic battle, approximately 35,000 Romans under Crassus were defeated by 9,000 Parthian horse archers and 1,000 cataphracts under Surena (Rustaham Suren-Pahlav). The outnumbered Roman cavalry were drawn off by the Parthian horse archers and defeated by the cataphracts. The unsupported Roman infantry were then subjected to a constant shower of arrows by the Parthian horse archers. Though well-armoured and protected by large shields, the Romans were unable to take any effective offensive action against the swift horse archers, and began to suffer severely from heat and thirst as well as lucky arrow shots. An attempt to advance against the Parthians achieved nothing. Eventually 20,000 Romans were killed and 10,000 more were later captured. They were relocated as military settlers in the east of the Parthian empire. There is a legend that they were later captured by the Han Chinese, and re-settled in China. There have been recent attempts to prove the truth of this legend using genetic testing.

Greek City Militia

PARTHIAN STARTER ARMY		
Commander-in-Chief	1	Surena (Inspired Commander)
Sub-commanders	2	2 x Troop Commander
Cataphracts	3 BGs	Each comprising 4 bases of cataphracts: Superior, Heavily Armoured, Undrilled Cataphracts – Lancers, Swordsmen
Horse Archers	7 BGs	Each comprising 4 bases of horse archers: Average, Unprotected, Undrilled Light Horse – Bow
Camp	1	Unfortified camp
Total	10 BGs	Camp, 40 mounted bases, 3 commanders

PARTHIAN

Parthian cataphract duelling with a Sassanid Persian cataphract, by Angus McBride. Taken from Men-at-Arms 175: Rome's Enemies (3) Parthians and Sassanid Persians.

BUILDING A CUSTOMISED LIST USING OUR ARMY POINTS

Choose an army based on the maxima and minima in the list below. The following special instructions apply to this army:

- Commanders should be depicted as cataphracts.
- Captured Seleucids cannot be used with Armenians or Saka.
- Indo-Parthians cannot have any allies except Saka.

PARTHIAN								
Territory Types: Agricultural, Steppes								
C-in-C	Inspired Commander/Field Commander/Troop Commander						80/50/35	1
Sub-commanders	Field Commander						50	0–2
	Troop Commander						35	0–3
Troop name	Troop Type				Capabilities		Points per base	Bases per BG	Total bases
	Type	Armour	Quality	Training	Shooting	Close combat			
Core Troops									
Cataphracts	Cataphracts	Heavily Armoured	Superior	Undrilled	–	Lancers, Swordsmen	18	4–6	6–18
Horse archers	Light Horse	Unprotected	Average	Undrilled	Bow	–	8	4–6	18–90
Optional Troops									
City militia or hill tribesmen	Light Foot	Unprotected	Average	Undrilled	Javelins	Light Spear	4	6–8	0–12
			Poor				2		
	Light Foot	Unprotected	Average	Undrilled	Bow	–	5	6–8	0–12
			Poor				3		
	Light Foot	Unprotected	Average	Undrilled	Sling	–	4	6–8	0–12
			Poor				2		
Greek city militia	All Medium Foot or all Heavy Foot	Protected	Poor	Drilled	–	Offensive Spearmen	6	6–8	0–8
Hillmen	Medium Foot	Protected	Average	Undrilled	–	Light Spear	5	6–8	0–8
Allies									
Adiabene, Edessan or Hatran allies									
Arab allies – Early Arab									
Armenian allies									
Commagene allies									
Elymaian allies									
Media-Atropatene allies									
Saka allies									
Special Campaigns									
Only Saka campaign in 129 BC									
Captured Seleucid pikemen	Heavy Foot	Protected	Poor	Drilled	–	Pikemen	4	8–12	0–12
Only Suren Indo-Parthian kingdom from 95 BC to 75 AD									
Hill tribe and Arachosian cavalry	Light Horse	Unprotected	Average	Undrilled	Javelins	Light Spear	7	4–6	0–6
Elephants	Elephants	–	Average	Undrilled	–	–	25	2	0–2
Indian levies	Medium Foot	Unprotected	Poor	Undrilled	Bow	–	3	6–12	0–12
Saka allies									

PARTHIAN OR MEDIA ATROPATENE ALLIES

Allied commander	Field Commander/Troop Commander						40/25	1	
Troop name	**Troop Type**				**Capabilities**		**Points per base**	**Bases per BG**	**Total bases**
	Type	Armour	Quality	Training	Shooting	Close combat			
Cataphracts	Cataphracts	Heavily Armoured	Superior	Undrilled	–	Lancers, Swordsmen	18	4–6	4–8
Horse archers	Light Horse	Unprotected	Average	Undrilled	Bow	–	8	4–6	6–24

ADIABENE, EDESSAN OR HATRAN ALLIES

Allied commander		Field Commander/Troop Commander						40/25	1	
Troop name		**Troop Type**				**Capabilities**		**Points per base**	**Bases per BG**	**Total bases**
		Type	Armour	Quality	Training	Shooting	Close combat			
Cataphracts		Cataphracts	Heavily Armoured	Superior	Undrilled	–	Lancers, Swordsmen	18	4	0–4
Cataphract camels	Only if Hatran	Camelry	Heavily Armoured	Superior	Undrilled	–	Lancers, Swordsmen	20	4	
Horse archers		Light Horse	Unprotected	Average	Undrilled	Bow	–	8	4–6	4–8
Foot archers		Light Foot	Unprotected	Average	Undrilled	Bow	–	5	6–8	6–24
		Medium Foot	Unprotected	Average	Undrilled	Bow	–	5	6–8	
Javelinmen		Light Foot	Unprotected	Average	Undrilled	Javelins	Light Spear	4	6–8	0–8
		Medium Foot	Protected	Average	Undrilled	–	Light Spear	5	6–8	

ELYMAIAN ALLIES

Allied commander	Field Commander/Troop Commander						40/25	1	
Troop name	**Troop Type**				**Capabilities**		**Points per base**	**Bases per BG**	**Total bases**
	Type	Armour	Quality	Training	Shooting	Close combat			
Cataphracts	Cataphracts	Heavily Armoured	Superior	Undrilled	–	Lancers, Swordsmen	18	4–6	4–6
Horse archers	Light Horse	Unprotected	Average	Undrilled	Bow	–	8	4–6	6–18
Foot archers	Light Foot	Unprotected	Average	Undrilled	Bow	–	5	6–8	0–16
	Medium Foot	Unprotected	Average	Undrilled	Bow	–	5	6–8	

COMMAGENE ALLIES

Commagene, north east of Cilicia and Syria, was a kingdom in its own right from 162 BC, when the Seleucid governor Ptolemy declared independence, until 72 AD, with brief interruptions during Tigran the Great's short-lived Armenian empire, and a period as a Roman province from 17 AD to 38 AD. After final annexation by Rome in 72 AD, the ruling family retired to Greece.

- The commander should be depicted as cataphracts.

COMMAGENE ALLIES								
Allied commander	Field Commander/Troop Commander					40/25		1
Troop name	Troop Type				Capabilities		Points per base	Bases per BG	Total bases
	Type	Armour	Quality	Training	Shooting	Close combat			
Cataphracts	Cataphracts	Heavily Armoured	Superior	Undrilled	-	Lancers, Swordsmen	18	4	0–4
Horse archers	Light Horse	Unprotected	Average	Undrilled	Bow	-	8	4–6	4–8
Foot archers	Light Foot	Unprotected	Average	Undrilled	Bow	-	5	6–8	6–24
	Medium Foot	Unprotected	Average	Undrilled	Bow	-	5	6–8	
Pikemen	Heavy Foot	Protected	Average	Drilled	-	Pikemen	6	8–12	8–12
			Poor				4		

EARLY ARAB ALLIES

Contingents of Arab tribesmen were often found as allies in the armies of the neighbouring states.

- The commander should be depicted as cavalry or light horse.

EARLY ARAB ALLIES								
Allied commander	Field Commander/Troop Commander					40/25		1
Troop name	Troop Type				Capabilities		Points per base	Bases per BG	Total bases
	Type	Armour	Quality	Training	Shooting	Close combat			
Cavalry	Light Horse	Unprotected	Average	Undrilled	Javelins	Light Spear	7	4–6	0–6
	Cavalry	Unprotected	Average	Undrilled	-	Light Spear, Swordsmen	8		
		Protected					9		
Camelry	Camelry	Unprotected	Poor	Undrilled	Bow	Swordsmen	10	4–6	0–8
Foot warriors	Medium Foot	Protected	Average	Undrilled	-	Light Spear, Swordsmen	6	6–8	0–16
Foot archers	Light Foot	Unprotected	Average	Undrilled	Bow	-	5	4–6	0–6
	Medium Foot	Unprotected	Average	Undrilled	Bow	-	5		

LATER SKYTHIAN OR SAKA ALLIES

The nomadic Scyths/Saka occupied much of the steppe from north of the Black Sea to north of Bactria. They have their own list in our book Field of Glory Companion 4: *Immortal Fire: Greek, Macedonian and Persian Wars*. This list covers Skythian or Saka allied contingents from 300 BC.

LATER SKYTHIAN OR SAKA ALLIES

Allied commander		Field Commander/Troop Commander						40/25		1	
Troop name		Troop Type				Capabilities		Points per base	Bases per BG	Total bases	
		Type	Armour	Quality	Training	Shooting	Close combat				
Armoured cavalry	Any	Cavalry	Armoured	Superior	Undrilled	-	Lancers, Swordsmen	16	4	0–4	
	Only Saka from 250 BC	Cataphracts	Heavily armoured	Superior	Undrilled	-	Lancers, Swordsmen	18	4		
Horse archers		Light Horse or Cavalry	Unprotected	Average	Undrilled	Bow	Swordsmen	10	4–6	6–18	
Foot archers		Light Foot	Unprotected	Average	Undrilled	Bow	-	5	6–8	0–8	
				Poor				3			
		Medium Foot	Unprotected	Average	Undrilled	Bow	-	5	6–8		
				Poor				3			
Foot spearmen		Medium Foot	Protected	Average	Undrilled	-	Light Spear	5	6–8	0–8	
				Poor				3			

LATER JEWISH

In 167 BC, Mattathias the Hasmonean, a Jewish priest, began a revolt against the Seleucid king Antiochos IV Epiphanes in response to decrees banning Jewish religious practice. His son Judah Maccabee led the Jewish rebels to victory over the Seleucid forces on several occasions, but was killed in the defeat of Elasa in 160 BC. His brothers Jonathan and Simon continued the fight, eventually securing Judaean independence and establishing the Hasmonean dynasty of Priest Kings. Civil wars and Roman intervention resulted in the replacement of the Hasmoneans by the Idumaean Herod the Great, who gained full control by 37 BC. He ruled as a Roman client until his death in 4 BC. The emperor Augustus divided his kingdom between his three sons: Herod Antipas in Galilee, Philip in the Golan heights region; and Herod Archelaus in Judaea (including Samaria and Idumaea). The latter ruled so badly that he was deposed by the Romans in 6 AD at the request of his subjects. Judaea became an autonomous part of the Roman province of Syria.

This list covers Jewish armies from 167 BC to 6 AD.

Emperor Augustus, Caesar's adopted heir.
(© R Sheridan/AAA Collection Ltd.)

THE WAR OF THE SONS OF LIGHT AGAINST THE SONS OF DARKNESS

This is the title of one of the Dead Sea Scrolls, also sometimes called the Rule of War. It describes an ideal army for an apocalyptic war against the unbelievers. The text has an obsession with the number 7, but describes the infantry as equipped with (7 cubit = approx 3 metres) long spear and (2.5 x 1.5 cubits = approx 1 metre x 0.67 metres) oval shield, forming up 7 ranks deep. Allowing for some adjustment to fit the magic number 7, this corresponds to the normal equipment and formation of Hellenistic thureophoroi. Slingers are also mentioned – they are expected to shoot 7 times then retire through the phalanx at a trumpet signal. The text concerning the cavalry is corrupt. There were clearly two types of cavalry, the older men (cavalry of the army) forming up in two large bodies (each of 700 men in 7 ranks) on each flank of the army, the younger (cavalry of the phalanx) in larger numbers but smaller squadrons (200 men) closely supporting the infantry. The cavalry of the phalanx wear helmet and greaves, carry a round shield and an 8-cubit (3.5 metre) lance. Bow and javelins are also mentioned, but due to the corruption of the text it is not clear which cavalry carry them. It could be that the Rule advocates the cavalry of the army carrying all these weapons, but it would be a reasonable assumption that bow and javelins might represent the (ideal) equipment of the cavalry of the phalanx.

Foot and Cavalry of the Phalanx with Cavalry of the Army

LATER JEWISH STARTER ARMY		
Commander-in-Chief	1	Field Commander
Sub-commanders	2	2 x Troop Commander
Cavalry of the army	1 BG	4 bases of cavalry: Superior, Armoured, Drilled Cavalry – Lancers, Swordsmen
Cavalry of the phalanx	2 BGs	Each comprising 4 bases of light horse: Average, Unprotected, Drilled Light Horse – Bow, Light Spear
Foot of the Phalanx	5 BGs	Each comprising 6 bases of thureophoroi: Average, Protected, Drilled Medium Foot – Offensive Spearmen
Javelinmen	1 BG	6 bases of javelinmen: Average, Unprotected, Undrilled Light Foot – Javelins, Light Foot
Archers	1 BG	8 bases of archers: Average, Unprotected, Undrilled Light Foot – Bow
Slingers	1 BG	8 bases of slingers: Average, Unprotected, Undrilled Light Foot – Sling
Camp	1	Unfortified camp
Total	11 BGs	Camp, 12 mounted bases, 52 foot bases, 3 commanders

BUILDING A CUSTOMISED LIST USING OUR ARMY POINTS

Choose an army based on the maxima and minima in the list below. The following special instructions apply to this army:

- Commanders should be depicted as cavalry of the army or cavalry of the phalanx.

- Non-upgraded foot of the phalanx or thureophoroi can be graded as Medium Foot or Heavy Foot, but all must be graded the same.
- Thracian horse must all be graded the same.
- The minimum marked * only applies if any cavalry other than commanders are used.

LATER JEWISH

Territory Types: Agricultural, Hilly

C-in-C	Inspired Commander/Field Commander/Troop Commander						80/50/35		1	
Sub-commanders	Field Commander						50		0–2	
	Troop Commander						35		0–3	
Troop name	**Troop Type**				**Capabilities**		**Points per base**	**Bases per BG**	**Total bases**	
	Type	Armour	Quality	Training	Shooting	Close Combat				
Core Troops										
Cavalry of the army or other xystophoroi	Cavalry	Armoured	Superior	Drilled	–	Lancers, Swordsmen	17	2–4	0–4	
Cavalry of the phalanx or other horse archers	Light Horse	Unprotected	Average	Drilled	Bow	Light Spear	9	4–6	0–12	
	Light Horse	Unprotected	Average	Drilled	Bow	–	8			
Foot of the phalanx or other thureophoroi	All Medium Foot or all Heavy Foot	Protected	Average	Drilled	–	Offensive Spearmen	8	6–8	*12–72	
Upgrade foot of the phalanx to pikemen	Only from 148 BC to 64 BC	Heavy Foot	Protected	Average	Drilled	–	Pikemen	6	8–12	0–24
Upgrade thureophoroi to Imitation Legionaries	Only from 63 BC	Heavy Foot	Protected	Average	Drilled	–	Impact Foot, Swordsmen	8	4–8	0–24
Javelinmen	Light Foot	Unprotected	Average	Undrilled	Javelins	Light Spear	4	6–8	6–32	
Archers	Light Foot	Unprotected	Average	Undrilled	Bow	–	5	6–8	6–32	
	Medium Foot	Unprotected	Average	Undrilled	Bow	–	5			
Slingers	Light Foot	Unprotected	Average	Undrilled	Sling	–	4	6–8	6–24	
Optional Troops										
Guerillas, hillmen, bandits or other levies	Medium Foot	Protected	Average	Undrilled	–	Light Spear	5	6–12	0–72 before 103 BC, 0–12 from 103 BC
		Unprotected	Average				4		
		Protected	Poor				3		
		Unprotected	Poor				2		
Replace xystophoroi or horse archers with Thracian horse	Only from 63 BC	Light Horse	Unprotected	Average	Undrilled	Javelins	Light Spear	7	4–6	0–8
		Cavalry	Armoured	Average	Drilled	–	Light Spear, Swordsmen	13		
Thracian foot	Only from 63 BC	Medium Foot	Protected	Average	Undrilled	–	Heavy weapon	7	6–8	0–8
					Drilled			8		
		Medium Foot	Protected	Average	Drilled	–	Light Spear, Swordsmen	7	6–8	
Fortified camp							24		0–1	

Allies								
Roman allies (Only from 63 BC) – Late Republican Roman or Principate Roman – See *Field of Glory Companion 5: Legions Triumphant: Imperial Rome At War*.								
Special Campaigns								
Only Hyrcanus II from 66 BC to 64 BC								
Nabataean allies								
Only from 48 BC to 47 BC								
Arab cavalry	Light Horse	Unprotected	Average	Undrilled	Javelins	Light Spear	7	4–6	0–6
	Cavalry	Unprotected	Average	Undrilled	–	Light Spear, Swordsmen	8		
		Protected					9		
Only Antigonus from 40 BC to 38 BC								
Parthian allies								

LATER JEWISH ALLIES

Allied commander		Field Commander/Troop Commander						40/25	1	
Troop name		**Troop Type**				**Capabilities**		Points per base	Bases per BG	Total bases
		Type	Armour	Quality	Training	Shooting	Close Combat			
Cavalry of the phalanx or other horse archers		Light Horse	Unprotected	Average	Drilled	Bow	Light Spear	9	4–6	0–6
		Light Horse	Unprotected	Average	Drilled	Bow	–	8		
Thracian horse	Only from 63 BC	Light Horse	Unprotected	Average	Undrilled	Javelins	Light Spear	7	4–6	
		Cavalry	Armoured	Average	Drilled	–	Light Spear, Swordsmen	13		
Foot of the phalanx or other thureophoroi		All Medium Foot or all Heavy Foot	Protected	Average	Drilled	–	Offensive Spearmen	8	6–8	6–18
Upgrade foot of the phalanx to pikemen	Only from 148 BC to 64 BC	Heavy Foot	Protected	Average	Drilled	–	Pikemen	6	8–12	0–12
Upgrade thureophoroi to Imitation Legionaries	Only from 63 BC	Heavy Foot	Protected	Average	Drilled	–	Impact Foot, Swordsmen	8	4–8	0–12
Javelinmen		Light Foot	Unprotected	Average	Undrilled	Javelins	Light Spear	4	6–8	6–12
Archers		Light Foot	Unprotected	Average	Undrilled	Bow	–	5	6–8	
		Medium Foot	Unprotected	Average	Undrilled	Bow	–	5		
Slingers		Light Foot	Unprotected	Average	Undrilled	Sling	–	4	6–8	

NABATAEAN ALLIES

The Nabataean kingdom in western Arabia became wealthy from trade. Its capital at Petra was (re)built in the latest Hellenistic style in the 1st century BC. The Nabateans fought both on the side of and against the Judaeans at various times, and also supplied client forces to the Romans.

- The commander should be depicted as Cavalry.

NABATAEAN ALLIES

Allied commander	Field Commander/Troop Commander						40/25		1
Troop name	**Troop Type**				**Capabilities**		**Points per base**	**Bases per BG**	**Total bases**
	Type	Armour	Quality	Training	Shooting	Close combat			
Cavalry	Cavalry	Armoured	Superior	Drilled	–	Lancers, Swordsmen	17	4	0–4
	Cavalry	Armoured	Superior	Drilled	–	Light Spear, Swordsmen	17	4	
Horse archers	Light Horse	Unprotected	Average	Undrilled or Drilled	Bow	–	8	4–6	4–8
Archers	Light Foot	Unprotected	Average	Undrilled	Bow	–	5	6–8	6–24
	Medium Foot	Unprotected	Average	Undrilled	Bow	–	5	6–8	
Upgrade archers to	Medium Foot	Unprotected	Average	Drilled	Bow	–	6	6–8	0–8
Javelinmen	Light Foot	Unprotected	Average	Undrilled	Javelins	Light Spear	4	6–8	0–8
	Medium Foot	Protected	Average	Undrilled	–	Light Spear	5	6–8	

BOSPORAN

Thracian Mercenary

This list covers the Bosporan kingdom on the north coast of the Black Sea from 348 BC to 375 AD: From Parysadas I until the kingdom fell to the Huns. From 108 BC to 63 BC, the Bosporan kingdom was under the rule of viceroys of Mithridates VI of Pontus. After his death, his successors continued to rule there until circa 10 AD. Thereafter it was a Roman client kingdom.

BOSPORAN STARTER ARMY

Commander-in-Chief	1	Field Commander
Sub-commanders	2	2 x Troop Commander
Lancers	2 BGs	Each comprising 4 bases of lancers: Superior, Armoured, Undrilled Cavalry – Lancers, Swordsmen
Horse archers	2 BGs	Each comprising 6 bases of horse archers: Average, Unprotected, Undrilled Light Horse – Bow, Swordsmen
Greek mercenary hoplites	2 BGs	Each comprising 6 bases of hoplites: Average, Protected, Drilled Heavy Foot – Offensive Spearmen
Thracian mercenaries	2 BGs	Each comprising 6 bases of Thracians: Average, Protected, Undrilled Medium Foot – Light Spear, Swordsmen
Maiotian javelinmen	1 BG	6 bases of javelinmen: Average, Unprotected, Undrilled Light Foot – Javelins, Light Spear
Maiotian archers	1 BG	8 bases of archers: Average, Unprotected, Undrilled Light Foot – Bow
Camp	1	Unfortified camp
Total	10 BGs	Camp, 20 mounted bases, 38 foot bases, 3 commanders

BUILDING A CUSTOMISED LIST USING OUR ARMY POINTS

Choose an army based on the maxima and minima in the list below. The following special instructions apply to this army:

- Commanders should be depicted as lancers.

- The minima marked * apply only if any city militia are used.
- Roman allies can omit otherwise compulsory legionaries or auxiliaries, but not both.

BOSPORAN									
Territory Types: Agricultural, Steppes									
C-in-C		Inspired Commander/Field Commander/Troop Commander					80/50/35	1	
Sub-commanders		Field Commander					50	0–2	
		Troop Commander					35	0–3	
Troop name		Troop Type				Capabilities		Points per base	Bases per BG	Total bases
		Type	Armour	Quality	Training	Shooting	Close Combat			
Core Troops										
Lancers	Before 108 BC	Cavalry	Armoured	Superior	Undrilled	–	Lancers, Swordsmen	16	4–6	4–12
			Protected					12		
	From 108 BC	Cavalry	Armoured	Superior	Undrilled	–	Lancers, Swordsmen	16	4–6	8–24
			Protected					12		
Horse archers	Before 108 BC	Light Horse or Cavalry	Unprotected	Average	Undrilled	Bow	Swordsmen	10	4–6	12–36
	From 108 BC									0–24
City militia	Any date	Medium Foot	Protected	Average	Drilled	–	Light Spear, Swordsmen	7	6–8	*6–12
			Armoured	Average				9		
			Protected	Poor				5		
	Only from 84 BC	Heavy Foot	Protected	Average	Drilled	–	Impact Foot, Swordsmen	8	4–8	
			Armoured	Average				10		
			Protected	Poor				6		
	Only from 42 AD	Medium or Heavy Foot	Protected	Average	Drilled	–	Light Spear, Swordsmen	7	4–8	
			Armoured	Average				9		
			Protected	Poor				5		
Sindi, Maiotian or other foot archers	Any date	Light Foot	Unprotected	Average	Undrilled	Bow	–	5	6–8	*6–24
				Poor				3		
		Medium Foot	Protected	Average	Undrilled	Bow	–	6	6–8	
		Medium Foot	Unprotected	Average	Undrilled	Bow	–	5	6–8	
				Poor				3		
	Only before 300 BC	Medium Foot	Unprotected	Average	Undrilled	Bow	Light Spear	5	1/2	6–8
							–	5	1/2	
Sindi, Maiotian or other javelinmen		Medium Foot	Protected	Average	Undrilled	–	Light Spear	5	6–8	*6–24
				Poor				3		
		Light Foot	Unprotected	Average	Undrilled	Javelins	Light Spear	4		
				Poor				2		

Optional Troops										
Slingers		Light Foot	Unprotected	Average	Undrilled	Sling	—	4	6–8	0–12
				Poor				2		
Greek mercenaries	Only before 11 AD	Heavy Foot	Protected	Average	Drilled	—	Offensive Spearmen	8	6–8	0–12
Thracian mercenaries	Only before 11 AD	Medium Foot	Protected	Average	Undrilled	—	Light Spear	5	6–8	0–12
	Only before 300 BC	Medium Foot	Protected	Average	Undrilled	—	Light Spear, Swordsmen	6		
	Only before 250 BC	Medium Foot	Protected	Average	Undrilled	—	Offensive Spearmen	7		
	Only before 11 AD	Medium Foot	Protected	Average	Undrilled	—	Heavy weapon	7		
Celtic mercenaries	Only from 108 BC to 10 AD	Heavy Foot	Protected	Average	Undrilled	—	Impact Foot, Swordsmen	7	6–8	
Bolt-shooters	Only from 42 AD	Heavy Artillery	—	Average	Drilled	Heavy Artillery	—	20	2	0–2
		Light Artillery	—	Average	Drilled	Light Artillery	—	17	2	
Ditch and bank	Only from 108 BC	Field Fortifications						3		0–24
Fortified camp								24		0–1

Allies
Sarmatian allies – Early Sarmatian – see Field of Glory Companion 4: *Immortal Fire: Greek, Persian and Macedonian Wars*
Skythian allies (Only before 11 AD) – Early Skythian or Saka allies – see Field of Glory Companion 3: *Immortal Fire: Greek, Persian and Macedonian Wars* – or Later Skythian or Saka allies
Roman allies (Only from 42 AD) – Principate Roman or Dominate Roman – see Field of Glory Companion 5: *Legions Triumphant: Imperial Rome At War*.

APPENDIX 1 – USING THE LISTS

To give balanced games, armies can be selected using the points system. The more effective the troops, the more each base costs in points. The maximum points for an army will usually be set at between 600 and 800 points for a singles game for 2 to 4 hours play. We recommend 800 points for 15mm singles tournament games (650 points for 25mm) and 1000 points for 15mm doubles games.

The army lists specify which troops can be used in a particular army. No other troops can be used. The number of bases of each type in the army must conform to the specified minima and maxima. Troops that have restrictions on when they can be used cannot be used with troops with a conflicting restriction. For example, troops that can only be used "before 235 BC" cannot be used with troops that can only be used "from 235 BC". All special instructions applying to an army list must be adhered to. They also apply to allied contingents supplied by the army.

All armies must have a C-in-C and at least one other commander. No army can have more

Thracian King Kotys and his bodyguards at the battle of Kallinikos, 171 BC, by Angus McBride.
Taken from Men-at-Arms 360: The Thracians 700 BC – AD 46.

than 4 commanders in total, including C-in-C, sub-commanders and allied commanders.

All armies must have a supply camp. This is free unless fortified. A fortified camp can only be used if specified in the army list. Field fortifications and portable defences can only be used if specified in the army list.

Allied contingents can only be used if specified in the army list. Most allied contingents have their own allied contingent list, to which they must conform unless the main army's list specifies otherwise.

BATTLE GROUPS

All troops are organized into battle groups. Commanders, supply camps and field fortifications are not troops and are not assigned to battle groups. Portable defences are not troops, but are assigned to specific battle groups.

Battle groups must obey the following restrictions:

- The number of bases in a battle group must correspond to the range specified in the army list.
- Each battle group must initially comprise an even number of bases. The only exception to this rule is that battle groups whose army list specifies them as $^2/_3$ of one type and $^1/_3$ of another, can comprise 9 bases if this is within the battle group size range specified by the list.

- A battle group can only include troops from one line in a list, unless the list specifies a mixed formation by specifying fractions of the battle group to be of types from two lines. e.g. $^2/_3$ spearmen, $^1/_3$ archers.
- All troops in a battle group must be of the same quality and training. When a choice of quality or training is given in a list, this allows battle groups to differ from each other. It does not permit variety within a battle group.
- Unless specifically stated otherwise in an army list, all troops in a battle group must be of the same armour class. When a choice of armour class is given in a list, this allows battle groups to differ from each other. It does not permit variety within a battle group.

EXAMPLE LIST

Here is a section of an actual army list, which will help us to explain the basics and some special features. The list specifies the following items for each historical type included in the army:

- Troop Type – comprising Type, Armour, Quality and Training.
- Capabilities – comprising Shooting and Close Combat capabilities.
- Points cost per base.
- Minimum and maximum number of bases in each battle group.
- Minimum and maximum number of bases in the army.

Troop name		Troop Type				Capabilities		Points per base	Bases per BG	Total bases	
		Type	Armour	Quality	Training	Shooting	Close Combat				
Xystophoroi	Only before 274 BC	Cavalry	Armoured	Superior	Drilled	–	Lancers, Swordsmen	18	4–6	4–6	
Javelin-armed heavy cavalry	Before 274 BC	Cavalry	Armoured	Superior	Drilled	–	Light Spear, Swordsmen	17	4–6	4–6	
				Average				14			
	From 274 BC	Cavalry	Armoured	Superior	Drilled	–	Light Spear, Swordsmen	17	4–6	6–12	
				Average				14			
Hoplites		Heavy Foot	Protected	Average	Drilled	–	Offensive Spearmen	8	6–8	0–18	
		Heavy Foot	Protected	Average	Undrilled	–	Offensive Spearmen	7			
				Poor				5			
Archers		Light Foot	Unprotected	Average	Drilled	Bow	–	5	6–8	0–12	
Slingers		Light Foot	Unprotected	Average	Drilled	Sling	–	4	6–8	0–12	6–18
Javelinmen		Light Foot	Unprotected	Average	Undrilled	Javelins	Light Spear	4	6–8	0–12	

Special features:
- Xystophoroi can only be used before 274 BC. Javelin-armed heavy cavalry can be used before or after 274 BC but the minimum and maximum numbers permitted change. Thus before 274, the army can and must include from 4 to 6 bases of xystophoroi and from 4 to 6 bases of javelin-armed heavy cavalry. From 274 BC the army cannot include any bases of xystophoroi but can and must include from 6 to 12 bases of javelin-armed heavy cavalry.
- Javelin-armed heavy cavalry can either be Superior or Average. The list specifies the different points costs. All the bases in a battle group must be of the same quality.

- Hoplites can be Average Drilled, Average Undrilled or Poor Undrilled. All the bases in a battle group must be of the same quality and training. The total number of hoplite bases in the army cannot exceed 18.
- The army is allowed from 0 to 12 bases each of archers, slingers and javelinmen. However, the total number of archers, slingers and javelinmen bases must be at least 6 and cannot exceed 18. Each battle group must have from 6 to 8 bases of one type – a battle group cannot include a mixture of archers and slingers or javelinmen.

APPENDIX 2 – THEMED TOURNAMENTS

A tournament based on the "Rise of Rome" theme can include any of the armies listed in this book.

It can also include the following armies from our other army list books. These can only use options permitted between 280 BC and 25 BC:

- Thracian
- Syracusan
- Galatian
- Hellenistic Greek
- Ancient British
- Early German

INDEX

Page numbers in **bold** refer to illustrations